Praise for *Choosing to*

MW01290156

"Many people die in circumstances they would never have chosen for themselves because their fear of death keeps them from learning about options available to them. Reading *Choosing to Die* will open your mind and heart. It will introduce you to the importance and possibility of a peaceful ending for yourself and your loved ones, and it is a fascinating story as well. It will also add to your understanding of grief and overcoming fear of death. Read it!"
—Trudy James, CEO and Producer of Heartwork: End of Life Planning Workshops, and Filmmaker for *Speaking of Dying*

"The story told in *Choosing to Die* is a harbinger of our culture's changing relationship with death and dying. Phyllis and Alan embody the emerging paradigm of couples, families, and friends embracing individual death as a shared experience through which all, the living and the dead, are united in a heightened awareness of life, love, and one another."
—John Wadsworth, Founding Editor and Creative Director of *Art of Dying* Magazine

"Phyllis Shacter is the one of the nation's most eloquent pioneers, spreading the word about one humane and legal way to negotiate life's final and sacred passage: Voluntarily Stopping Eating and Drinking. Her story of her husband's last nine and a half days will help many others retain their autonomy in the face of degenerative disease and find their way to a peaceful, good end of life."
—Katy Butler, author of *Knocking on Heaven's Door: The Path to a Better Way of Death* and *A Good End of Life: A Practical Guide*

"In *Choosing to Die*, Phyllis Shacter offers her readers an indispensable guide to previously uncharted waters in end-of-life care. Inspired by her husband Alan's heartfelt wish to have

his own experience benefit others, Phyllis tells a story of true love while delivering a compelling and practical account of the joys and difficulties of facing illness and death with eyes wide open. For people with terminal illness, their families, and all who care for them, including hospice, *Choosing to Die* illuminates a world of challenges and possibilities with clarity and grace."
—Hope Wechkin, MD, is the Medical Director at Evergreen Health Hospice and Palliative Care, Kirkland, WA

"With courage, commitment and compassion Phyllis Shacter tells the story of her husband's death by VSED and her own grief process. She leads us through the seemingly terrifying journey of Alan's last days and reveals instead the gentle beauty, peace, and healing that resulted from his heroic choice. As a result, the reader's own fear of death is dispelled with the turning of each page. This book is both a clarion call to rethink our approach to dying and death and a step-by-step guide for those who are brave enough to follow the path forged with great love by Alan and Phyllis. Read this book to learn about VSED as an option at the end of life, to be inspired by Alan's story of conscious living and dying, and moreover to explore the breadth of love between two people that ultimately transcends all suffering."
—Karen M. Wyatt, MD, Hospice Physician, Spiritual Teacher, Speaker, and author of the Award-Winning Book, *What Really Matters*

"A must read for individuals with incurable serious illness and those helping them. When faced with intractable physical or existential suffering, some patients decide to hasten their deaths. This book will help ensure that choice is voluntary and informed, by empowering you and your family about one increasingly important exit option: voluntarily stopping eating and drinking. Written with warmth, sensitivity, and tact, the author details her personal experience both before, during, and after her husband stopped eating and drinking. She thereby provides practical guidance for others navigating similar legal,

clinical, and emotional hurdles."
—Thaddeus Mason Pope, JD, PhD, Director of the Health Law Institute and Professor of Law, Mitchell Hamline School of Law

"In *Choosing to Die*, Phyllis Shacter gives us an intensely personal as well as medically well-informed account of her husband's choice to die by VSED to avoid living years into severe dementia. Shacter provides others' accounts as well as her own, including an exemplary and revealing day-by-day record of Alan's path to death by one of his nurses. *Choosing to Die* is a uniquely helpful, close-up, this-is-what-it's-like view of VSED."
—Paul T. Menzel, Professor of Philosophy Emeritus, Pacific Lutheran University, Tacoma, WA

"*Choosing to Die* is a personal yet comprehensive guide to Voluntary Stopping Eating and Drinking (VSED). VSED is an important option at end-of-life and this book helps fill the knowledge gap it currently experiences. Shacter's willingness to share her most intimate experiences, feelings, and insights as she journeys with her husband when he chose VSED can only benefit others who may want to consider this option."
—Anne Koepsell, former executive director of Washington State Hospice & Palliative Care Organization.

A Personal Thank You to Phyllis and Alan
"My husband began his ten-day journey on December 5, 2016. He had the gentle, peaceful death we had all been hoping for. We never could have done this without you and the additional support of End of Life Washington. Please know that the work you are doing to increase awareness of this option is so important. In sharing my husband's decision and his journey with friends, I have received nothing but support and admiration for the choice he made and the courage he showed in carrying out his wish." —A Grateful Family

CHOOSING TO DIE

A Personal Story

Elective Death by Voluntarily Stopping Eating and Drinking (VSED) in the Face of Degenerative Disease

by
PHYLLIS SHACTER

Foreword by
Timothy E. Quill MD, FACP, FAAHPM

DISCOUNTS OR CUSTOMIZED EDITIONS MAY BE AVAILABLE FOR EDUCATIONAL AND OTHER GROUPS BASED ON BULK PURCHASE.

For further information please contact:
Phyllis Shacter, info@PhyllisShacter.com

For Alan

Magical man who is so gentle,
Weaving your inner magic into fluid forms.
You find joy and discovery in all that you do.

From a lone computer programmer,
To a famous consultant entrepreneur,

From of dreamer of NLP
To a Master Practitioner of the trade.

From a ballroom dancer,
To an expressive weaver of life.

From a classical piano student,
To an improvisational jazz performer.

From Harvard, to the professor you've been,
You continue to grow and learn for the long term.

From layers of form in all that you do,
To your soulful embrace of Life.

Magical man, who is so gentle,
It's your gentleness that makes you so special.

Gentle man
Gentle husband
Gentle father
Son, brother and friend.

You have a soft melody that sings through you.
I love your song.

I love you.

Love Rains, Reigns, Remains

CONTENTS

FOREWORD

Of all the illnesses to die from in this life, Alzheimer's, ALS, Parkinson's and other degenerative diseases have to be among the most daunting. The amount of time from initial diagnosis to eventual death is measured in years rather than months. The prognosis is so long and so uncertain that hospice, the premiere program designed to help provide comfort and dignity at the end of life, is not available until the very last stages. Patients with these diseases eventually become completely dependent upon others, so the shattering impact is on families as well as patients. Is there any way to escape the suffering and indignities that these diseases inevitably create?

This was the challenge faced by Alan Alberts. In this remarkable book, his wife Phyllis gives us an inside look at one couple's effort to come to grips with and take charge of a devastating diagnosis.

Alan was diagnosed with Alzheimer's. He wanted to live as long as he could remain cognitively intact and, to at least some degree, be in charge of his life. But he also wanted to escape the long relentless decline and complete loss of self associated with the late stages of Alzheimer's disease—even if it meant hastening his death. Together Alan and Phyllis explored whether he could have access to a physician assisted death, and learned that even though he lived in one of the six states in the U.S.A. where this practice is currently legal, he would not qualify because his prognosis was too long and uncertain. They then discovered the possibility of voluntarily stopping eating and drinking (VSED for short), a process where a seriously ill patient, at a time of his or her own choosing, makes a decision to completely stop eating and drinking in a deliberate effort to hasten death. Alan decided that VSED was his best option.

This book offers readers an inside look at the many challenges leading up to, carrying out, and then making sense afterward of this decision. Phyllis walks the reader through every step, from Alan's initial diagnosis, to searching for options for escape, to learning about VSED as a last resort option, to deciding when to begin the process, to carrying out the final phase, to experiencing profound bereavement, and to gradually picking up the pieces of her life after Alan's death. VSED is not a journey for the faint of heart (but then, neither is prolonged degenerative disease). VSED is filled with times of intense intimacy and disconnection, with caregivers and friends, including those who step up and help and those who are frightened or disapproving. Phyllis's book does not shy away from the hard parts of Alan's story, as well as the parts that were uplifting and inspiring.

Of all the "last resort" options for elective death— including physician-assisted death, voluntary euthanasia, palliative sedation, and stopping life-sustaining therapies —VSED is the least well-described or understood by the general public. This valuable, groundbreaking book fills that gap, and is invaluable reading for any patient and family seriously considering embarking on VSED—whether soon, because of a current condition of unacceptable suffering, or for some time in the far-off future, for those exploring the full range of legally available end-of-life options. The aging of the population due to advances in public health and medical treatments means that the number of people who will eventually develop degenerative diseases will increase. If you read this compelling and informative story now, you will forever after know that VSED exists, should you or any loved one ever be in a position to need it as an option.

One of the best aspects of this book is that Phyllis is not overly romantic about her story, nor is she overly negative. This book is full to the brim of practical wisdom learned through experience—critical information for anyone who is now contemplating or might ever consider the option of VSED. The book contains no shortage of dilemmas that do not have easy answers. What is the right time to initiate the process? How does one avoid starting too early given the risk of waiting until it is too late? How much decision-making capacity does the patient need to make this decision? How do caregivers manage the patient's desire to drink when the patient no longer remembers why he or she is not drinking? Can we offer this option to patients who do not have an advocate like Phyllis to organize and provide the care? Is it realistic to do this at home for patients who do not have the psychological, social, and financial resources that Alan and Phyllis had? Should VSED be permitted and supported in inpatient palliative care or hospice units? Should all seriously ill patients be informed about this option, or do they have to discover it on their own?

None of these questions has an easy answer, nor does Phyllis pretend to solve all such dilemmas in this book. Instead she has openly and compassionately described her VSED journey with Alan so that we can learn from her experience.

If you worry about how to potentially shape the last

phase of your life in the distant future, or if you are actively looking at last resort options to escape very challenging clinical problems right now, this book is a must-read. It is filled with practical wisdom, advice, and realism about the challenges and potential of VSED from a couple who found this a meaningful way to end life's journey when faced with an irreversible medical problem.

—*Dr. Timothy E. Quill MD, FACP, FAAHPM*
February 4, 2017

CHAPTER ONE
Why You Need to Know About VSED

Introduction

My beloved husband of twenty-six years, Alan, decided to die by Voluntarily Stopping Eating and Drinking (VSED) rather than live into the late stages of Alzheimer's disease. He watched his mother deteriorate from Alzheimer's for more than ten years until she was a shadow of a person with no physical or mental capacities. Alan knew he did not want to experience that horror and die a person unrecognizable from his real, former self. We learned that VSED is a legal option, and Alan decided to do it, grateful that he had found an alternative.

From a place of deep sadness, yet buoyed by the strength and commitment of our love for one another and of his commitment to this process, I became my husband's advocate so he could VSED. Alan was loved and cherished up to his last breath. He left his body as consciously as he lived his life. I was privileged to be his friend and wife for twenty-six years, and was his advocate every step of the way. Considering the circumstances, our experience was positive in many ways. Alan wanted other people to know about VSED, and I became committed to letting everyone know that VSED is a safe, legal, comfortable alternative to months or years of suffering and low quality of life.

For the weeks leading up to the date that Alan had decided to begin his fast, we cried together virtually every day. He remained steadfast in his decision. I did all I could think of to set up a safe and supportive environment so that Alan could go through his process with me by his side, loving him every step of the way. It was the most difficult thing I've ever had to do. Alan's clarity about his decision, all the information I had gathered, and our knowledge that he was doing the right thing, kept me focused.

Once Alan began his fast, it took him nine and a half days to die. He died on April 19, 2013. I was able to communicate with him until the eighth day. On that day, he could no longer open his eyes, but he was still aware. I got very close to him and said, "Alan, I am here with you. If you are comfortable, blink your eyes." His eyes were closed, but he was able to move his eyelids, and I knew he was okay and not suffering. While he was in that state, he mouthed his last words to me, "I love you."

On the ninth day, soon after midnight, our caregiver woke me up because she noticed a big shift in Alan. She felt he was getting close to his death. Immediately, I crawled into his small hospital bed with him. His breathing was labored and loud. I couldn't relax, but stayed with him until 5:30 a.m. when I could hear the birds singing. I went back to my own bed. I knew I needed some sleep because he was going to die soon, and people would be coming to the house. I was exhausted.

About noon, the doctor arrived for her regular visit. When she examined Alan, she said that he was "brain dead" and that there was only a little activity left in his brain stem. He was still breathing, and she said that his heart was strong and that he would probably live another one to three days.

I was disturbed. In my deep intuition, I felt that Alan

was ready to release himself and to leave completely, and I didn't want him to suffer. Talking privately with our doctor, I asked her to give him a dose of medication that would allow him to let go and die. But she would not do this. Soon after, she left the house.

So, I spontaneously drew on whatever resources I could think of to help him. Having been trained in Therapeutic Touch, an energy healing modality that I learned from nurses in the 1990s, I used it to vigorously move energy from the top of his head down through the whole length of his body and out the window near his feet.

I began to talk to Alan. The words came spontaneously. It almost felt like a pep talk. "Alan, we've partnered together for twenty-six years. We did everything together in our business, with our families, with our life. I might orchestrate something, but then we'd carry it out together. This is our last partnership. I'm going to help you. You can let go now. You've done all your work. You're so courageous. You're going to get your wish. You're not going to have to live into the late stages of Alzheimer's. There's nothing left that you have to do. It's time for you to go."

I thought I was finished. I stood silently by his bed. Then I began to sing a sacred chant that we both knew. I sang it over and over and over and continued gently with the Therapeutic Touch, helping to move the energy out of his body. He became very quiet; his loud rattling breath subsided. He opened his mouth in a circular wide motion and took a couple of very gentle slow breaths, so gentle that I couldn't detect the last breath. He left.

He did not live for another one to three days as the doctor had predicted. With me close by his side, talking to him and loving him, he left his body in less than fifteen minutes.

This book is our story. I will relate our experience in

detail because I am deeply committed to making VSED more widely known and understood. So many people in circumstances similar to ours—or with other degenerative diseases—can be spared terrible and prolonged suffering if they know that VSED is an end-of-life option, that it is legal, and that, with the proper medical support, the dying person can be kept comfortable.

Elective death, by the Death with Dignity Act or by VSED may not be the choice everyone would make. I have a deep respect for other people's beliefs and religious convictions and would never presume to recommend VSED unless a person requests information. I am telling our story to make accurate information about VSED accessible to anyone who is curious about it.

In this book, I will describe our decision process; the legal, medical, physical, and spiritual preparations we made; the resistance we encountered and how we managed it; and the nine and a half days it took Alan to die once he started to VSED. We decided to make our experience public throughout the process of Alan's illness and while we made important decisions, and to deliberately employ our experience to pave the way for others.

As I will explain at length in Chapter Six, this entire experience has transformed my own debilitating fear of death. This remarkable gift, to be freed of my fear, is an outcome I did not anticipate or expect and is another reason I am committed to sharing our story. I hope diminished fear will be an outcome for others who make this courageous journey.

VSED is not new. In quiet corners, for years, people have stopped eating and drinking when they felt it was their time to die. What *is* new is that VSED no longer needs to be kept secret, and that legal, medical, psychological, and spiritual help is increasingly available to assist people who want a conscious and deliberate way to avoid the late stages of debilitating diseases and the indignities and suffering that accompany them. My goal with this book is to make useful information more widely available.

What About the Death with Dignity Act?

It is true that several states have passed the Death with Dignity Act. This law allows a person to self-administer a lethal drug under certain specific circumstances. However, the Death with Dignity Act states that in order to self-administer the drug legally, a person must be mentally competent and in the last six months of life. When Alzheimer's patients are in the last six months of life, they are not mentally competent. Death with Dignity laws are a wonderful option for people with cancer and some other terminal diseases, but their restrictive guidelines render them useless for patients with Alzheimer's and most other neurological diseases. And of course, in many states, voluntary death by a lethal drug is not yet legal. Some people consider using this method anyway, by accumulating drugs and using them to overdose. But this is risky, especially if it encourages loved ones to engage in illegal activities. This is why widespread knowledge about the option of VSED is critically important.

There is another significant distinction between the Death with Dignity Act—that is, self-administering a prescribed lethal drug—and VSED. My husband, while he was still mentally competent, said that he preferred to stop eating and drinking even if he could have qualified for the Death with Dignity Act because he wanted to experience a more natural, organic death, and allow his body to break down and die. He wanted to be present as long as he could, and be conscious while he was dying. Also, if the Death with Dignity Act had been available to us, I would have had a more difficult time as his wife. To have him fully here, and then lose consciousness in ten to fifteen minutes would have been too great a shock for me. His death was easier for me to accept because I watched it happen over nine and a half days. It was something we did together, something we shared, a gift that has remained with me in all the months and years since.

Is VSED Suicide?

When Alan made his decision to VSED, some people worried, "Is he committing suicide?" This is a legitimate question, and I believe it is important for the VSED movement to be careful about our language. Personally, I would like the word "suicide" to be eliminated from our vocabulary when we speak of VSED or Death with Dignity. These are not "suicides," but rather, "elective deaths." Suicide is secretive, often violent, outside the natural order, woefully ill considered, and usually devastating to others. It is saying a giant NO to life. By contrast, Alan was saying YES to life, up to his last breath, on his terms. His death was peaceful and completely in rhythm with the natural order. It was a deeply considered decision based on self-love, peace, and compassion, for himself and for those around him. Alan's plan and decision was not secretive, but shared with many who loved him. He died, not alone, but surrounded by love. He was grateful for the good life he had lived and grateful to have the choice to VSED.

There is a world of difference between suicide and elective death. All people who thoughtfully pursue elective death should be granted the respect of terminology that distinguishes their choice from the sudden, often horrifying, ill-considered, negative choice of suicide.

Others asked if Alan was dying prematurely. It is true, Alan did give up some time and some quality of life in order to have a good quality of death. His VSED process could not be timed perfectly. But he was absolutely certain he did not want to live into the late stages of Alzheimer's, so this sacrifice was more than worth it to him. He timed his elective death as well as he could.

How Does VSED Affect Life Insurance?

Many people have asked me if life insurance applies if someone decides to VSED. Based on my research, it appears that it depends on when the policy was purchased. If it was purchased more than one year before the death, then the "suicide" exclusion clause in the life insurance policy should not apply. Anyone who is considering VSED and owns a life insurance policy should consult that company's policy.

The Dread of Lingering Degenerative Diseases

We all know of truly horrible stories that could have been avoided if VSED had been a known alternative. My mother took care of my father through heart disease, prostate cancer, and Alzheimer's. She had been participating in an Alzheimer's caregivers' support group already for several years. When my father was in the late stages of Alzheimer's, I received an emergency phone call from my mother. "Please get on a plane. I need you here right away. I can't take care of your father anymore." She was 80 and he was 83. This occurred right after my first date with Alan, and he drove me to the airport.

When I arrived, I learned that my mother had been sleeping in the second bedroom and was barricading the door at night with furniture in case my father tried to come in to harm her. He had threatened her on two occasions, and she called 911 each time. By the time the police arrived, my father was asleep on the couch completely unaware of what was going on. This can be the nature of this cruel disease. It was 1987, and we placed my father in a board and care home where he died seven months later due to complications with pneumonia. My mother came to live with Alan and me. She had devoted more than eight years to caring for someone so diseased that he was a danger to her. VSED might have spared them both the agonies of many of those eight years.

Sometimes, the courts themselves are the biggest obstacle to justice and peace. In a story reported in the *Vancouver Sun* on November 11, 2016, an eighty-five-year old woman in Canada, Margot Bentley, finally died after lingering in a vegetative state and a rigid body from Alzheimer's for more than seventeen years. Her life was prolonged at the nursing home even though Margot, a nurse herself, had written a living will in 1991 saying she did not want to live if she incurred an incurable disease and could not feed herself. Her daughter tried to honor her mother's wishes. But misguided courts took all the power away from Margot's daughter, and expressly prohibited her from removing her mother from the nursing facility to take her home to die. This woman tragically became a figure in a "right-to-die case" that her daughter bravely fought in the courts—and lost.

When Alan's mother was suffering in the early stages of Alzheimer's, on two separate occasions, she said she would like to take an overdose of pills so she would not have to endure the indignities she knew were ahead for her. But she feared the pills might not work and that her attempt would leave her in an even worse vegetative state. After ten years, she died of Alzheimer's when she was left with no physical or mental capacities. Alan told me that he felt his mother would have chosen VSED if she knew about it at the time, and if she could have been supported through the process. Alan was absolutely certain he would not put himself through those years of agony he saw his mother endure.

Most adults have heard someone say facetiously, "If I ever get Alzheimer's, just shoot me!" People say this because they know the horror of the disease, and they don't know what else to say. I even heard a well-known doctor say this! Many diseases have offered no dignified exit—until now, when the Death with Dignity Act and VSED have become more widely known alternatives.

You may know someone who was genuinely ready to die but had no way to make it happen. The person had an incurable disease, was in constant pain, had incipient dementia, or in some other way, had lost virtually all quality of life and all hope of ever recovering it. The person was restless and unhappy and enormously frustrated, as were all the people trying hard to support him or her.

Before I lived through the experience I will describe in this book, I did not know that every diseased person has the fully legal option of deciding how and when to die, simply by deciding to stop eating and drinking, surrounded by medical supervision and loving support. We each have the choice to preclude months or years of suffering and pain, and to avoid putting our beloved families through years of painful caretaking.

In the same way we orchestrate our birthdays and weddings, we can orchestrate our departure from this world. After Alan's death, people came forward to tell us that they saw great dignity in his death and that they saw VSED as an expression of his civil rights. Many people expressed deep relief knowing that this option is available to them someday if necessary.

My Commitment to VSED Education

Two weeks before Alan began his fast, he was sitting at the breakfast table. I was standing nearby and noticed that he was crying. "Honey," I said, "Why are you crying? What are you feeling?"

He replied, "I'm not afraid of dying; I've lived a good life. But I want everyone to know about VSED!"

I heard myself say "You'll just have to trust that I'll be your vehicle for spreading the information." Then, I heard myself gasp, wondering what I had just committed myself to.

I am carrying out my promise to my husband because I witnessed the peace and even joy that came over him, once he had made his decision to VSED. I saw and was a part of his peaceful end, and the entire experience transformed my own perspective about death. After a deep grieving process, and missing my husband intensely, I emerged to find peace, meaning, and gratitude in my life. I'm sharing our story because so many people already face or will face the same kinds of sadness, fear, and bewilderment that we struggled through. In our case, we had no guidelines. We blazed a trail through an uncharted forest of questions and fears. I believe that our story will provide hope and guidance for others in circumstances similar to ours. Knowledge and accurate information alleviate anxiety. Also, a prime motivation for me is my hope that the facts I provide will motivate doctors, hospice organizations, caregivers, and health professionals to be compassionate and supportive as their patients consider end-of-life options in distressing circumstances.

Shortly after our experience and after Alan died, I learned that the TEDx talks were coming to our town. I applied and was selected to give a presentation about how and why my husband decided to VSED. Only seven months after Alan died, I bravely stood before a live audience of 135 people and shared our story, through my sadness and tears. (This talk can be found on the home page of my website, www.PhyllisShacter.com.) That talk became the first of many public presentations I have made since. I continue to speak at conferences and other events, and have been interviewed on the radio, Internet, and for newspapers and magazines.

My website contains detailed information about our story and about VSED. I helped to organize and speak at the first National Conference on VSED at Seattle University in October 2016. Our story is reaching many thousands of people, and I am learning how surprised and grateful people are to learn that VSED exists, that it is legal, and that, when properly supported, it can be a good end of life option. Alan's desire to make the general public aware of the option of VSED and to make accurate information more widely available is occurring.

For twelve years, starting in the late 1980s, Alan and I worked together in our own consulting partnership, assisting law firms to become more profitable and effective by using appropriate hardware and software. Alan was the technology expert, and I contributed business expertise. We loved working together and valued the opportunity to stretch ourselves and to grow and learn. Laughter, mostly toward ourselves and each other, punctuated every day. We thrived in each other's presence.

In the early 1990s, once a week in the evening, we watched a television program called "Touched by an Angel" starring Della Reese. She was an angel who was given an assignment on earth every week to improve someone's life. Every week, we watched this program together in bed and often cried at the poignancy of these "assignments." Now, it seems obvious that Alan and I have been given an assignment in our own lives. He was exemplary in carrying out his part. We talked together about every decision and every step of the process. After he died, I became the vehicle to carry out his request to share with the world information that we hope will diminish the fear of dying for others.

Does it give you comfort, right now, to know that you have the option to avoid a lingering disease and to know that a peaceful, orchestrated death is an option for you if the circumstances warrant it? My hope is that the information in this book enables you to embrace life fully—now, in the present—with added peace and gratitude.

CHAPTER TWO
Our VSED Story

Our Life Before Alzheimer's

Alan and I had friends in common and had known each other slightly before we became a couple. Our stories about each other were distorted in ways we later laughed about. But when we came together for our first genuine conversation in February 1987, I could feel myself relax and take a long exhalation. It was so easy to talk with and be around Alan. He had a quiet, introverted composure that balanced my extroversion and high energy. We were both single, and we both wanted to be in a relationship. It was during that first conversation that I knew we would be together until one of us died. I was thirty-nine; Alan, forty-nine. We had both been married before. We each had one daughter, and we were both ready for a change in our lives. Several years into our relationship, to our great delight, we realized that Alan had been my Teaching Assistant at the University of California at Berkeley when I was seventeen and he was twenty-seven.

We decided to start our own small business. Alan had taken the first computer course ever given in the world at Harvard University, had been in the computer field for his entire career, and had also attended law school. I had taught school and then worked on a creative sales team and learned about consultative selling. I did in depth needs assessments and came up with creative solutions. The perfect combination of our skills was to assess lawyers' needs and enhance their productivity by introducing them to appropriate legal hardware and software and teaching them to use it.

Even though we were in a new relationship, we trusted and respected each other's skills. At the same time that we launched both our relationship and our new business, we moved to a new city and invited my healthy 84-year-old mother to live with us. It was a lot of change in a short period of time, and it went well. We felt like twenty-three year olds involved in our first career. It was a very exciting time for us.

Starting a new business was definitely stressful. We discovered as we went along that our antidote to stress was our mutual propensity to laugh at ourselves and each other. We didn't get caught up in the multitude of details, the long hours we worked, or our steep learning curve. Instead, when we encountered a challenge, we'd break into hysterical laughter. We'd make mistakes and we'd laugh. We'd feel anxious, and we'd laugh. Alan wasn't the best communicator, and when he fumbled, we'd laugh (later)! I recall one time when he told a client that he didn't have to pay us yet. I kicked Alan lightly under the table, interrupted him, and said we would like to be paid that day! When we left the office, we were breathless with laughter. People around us had no idea what was so funny! It was a magical part of our relationship.

Here is another example: When we visited a client in the early days of our business, as we were getting out of the car, I noticed that my genius husband was wearing the jacket of one suit, and the pants of another. But instead of becoming upset and concerned about our image, we broke into uncontrollable laughter. We both leaned on the hood of the car so we wouldn't fall over. Once we calmed down, we went into the appointment, with Alan's jacket over his arm, acting like nothing had happened. These types of things happened to us over and over again. It was our laughter that kept us afloat. Rarely did a day go by where we didn't share a deep belly laugh about something.

Besides having the gift of laughter, which was a profound way for us to communicate, we also partnered in another deep way. Alan started playing the piano when he was nine years old and loved to improvise. I had played classical piano since I was four but was always envious of people who could improvise. Sixteen years after we were together, Alan gave me a book about improvisation, about how it was possible to let the music flow from one's unconscious mind to the conscious mind. During one of our conversations about improvisation, I sat down at our piano and my hands began to move, first in a very elementary way. We had both an electronic keyboard and an acoustic piano, and soon, improvising together was our deepest form of communication. One of us would play a note, the other would listen and respond and soon we'd be playing together. We even played for others. We made beautiful music together up to the last weeks of Alan's life. I felt honored when he told me that I was his favorite improvisation partner, because he had played with some famous people in his day! I've played the piano very little since he died. At first, it was too painful because of all the beautiful memories. I wonder if I'll ever be able to play again with another keyboard player.

It seemed that we were always creating together as a way of loving each other. Alan fulfilled a childhood dream when he learned how to do magic tricks. Then I began to partner with him again. I'd research and write magical stories about people's lives, and Alan would perform magic tricks that tied into the theme of the stories. We performed at parties. People even paid us to do this! We put on costumes, created accents, and played together—just another activity that resulted in plenty of laughter.

Early Signs of Alzheimer's

We moved from California to Washington in 2004, two years after my mother died. Alan was sixty-eight years old. He began to have a lot less stamina. I knew there was neurological disease hovering in the background. Alan's mother died of Alzheimer's. His father had significant memory problems even though his death was caused by colon cancer. My father also died of Alzheimer's.

When I was forty and Alan was fifty, we each filled out our Health Directives and wrote a Will. My huge fear, tucked in the recesses of my mind, was that he would get Alzheimer's someday, because I knew his family history. I never mentioned my fear to Alan. Instead I became fanatical about encouraging him to take good care of himself.

Two years after we moved to Washington, Alan began to have medical issues. First we learned that he had an HPV viral wart on his right vocal cord. It compromised his voice, and he could feel the growth. He had to have it removed with a laser about every three months. Then he began to feel more tired, and for a few years, we went from one medical specialist to another trying to learn why Alan felt so tired. No one had an answer. He began to sleep more and more. He also had some thyroid issues, sleep apnea, and his blood sugar was increasing.

Then I noticed that Alan was becoming less attentive when driving, and I told him that I wanted to do all the driving when we were in the car. I noticed financial files in different places, and I took over all the financial details for our household. In addition to his fatigue, I noticed that he was more forgetful, not just with people's names, but leaving drawers open where someone could fall, and leaving the heat on the stovetop. When he was at the computer working and I interrupted him, he became upset because he couldn't easily return to his project. Something as simple as putting staples into a stapler became a challenge. These were all early signs of Alzheimer's, but we didn't know it yet.

Alan continued to have short-term memory loss. We both agreed it would be a good idea for him to be examined by a neuropsychologist. The same doctor saw him in both 2007 and in 2009. He gave him two hours of cognitive tests that used different parts of his brain. Both times, the doctor said he was fine.

During a six-month period in 2011, Alan had pneumonia twice. One of those times, I had to call 911 because he couldn't move and he was very confused.

In November 2011, he was examined again by a neuropsychologist. This time he was diagnosed with "dementia of the Alzheimer's type." By this time, there was a noticeable decline in Alan's short-term attention and concentration. Given the medical tools of the day, it was not possible to diagnose Alan's Alzheimer's when he was in the earlier stages.

We both felt it was best if Alan did not take any medications relating to the diagnosis. There would be side effects, and virtually nothing could be done to mitigate the disease. Six weeks later, he was also diagnosed with laryngeal cancer. The area where the HPV viral wart had been removed many times became cancerous. Since the cancer needed immediate attention, we focused on that and went into Alzheimer's denial.

Alan was seeing a naturopath in the greater Seattle area. I became like a drill sergeant making sure he took all his supplements and followed all the prescribed procedures.

Because he had Alzheimer's, I had to stand by his side and make sure he did everything correctly from morning to night. My days started early and went to late at night. I was exhausted and grief stricken. I was committed to helping Alan with whatever he needed. My love for him was very deep.

I wanted to grow old with Alan. He was my best friend. My vision was that we would die when we were both old. But this wasn't to be our fate. Instead I kept putting one foot in front of the other and became an excellent advocate, fully committed to helping Alan with whatever he needed. It was this focus that kept me from collapsing.

In Chapter Five, I will share the story of how Alan healed his cancer in four months. When the cancer was gone, we thought he might still have a few good years ahead of him. But the Alzheimer's quickly became more aggressive. There was one week when it was so obvious that his memory was getting worse, we just held each other and cried most of that week.

Finally, we faced up fully to the Alzheimer's diagnosis. What were we going to do? We felt desperate. Were there any alternatives to a dementia facility like the one his mother had experienced? Alan could not stand the thought of that.

Making the Decision to VSED

I sought the guidance of an organization called "End of Life Washington," the organization that sponsored the Death with Dignity Act in Washington State. The volunteer chaplain there told me about VSED. It was the first time I had ever heard about or known to even consider such a thing. I was both shocked and intrigued. She suggested I do some legal research about this. I found an article online by Thaddeus Pope and Lindsey Anderson, "Voluntarily Stopping Eating and Drinking: A Legal Treatment Option

At The End of Life." I read and copied this article and gave it to Alan to read. After he read it, he said, "I've read this paper, and I've decided I'm going to VSED." This occurred six months before he actually went through the VSED process. However, to make absolutely certain about his choice, we knew that we needed to rule out all other options.

Another possibility for the late stages of his disease was a facility for Alzheimer's patients. So we decided to visit one.

I picked the most expensive facility in our county, thinking it would be the nicest. In 2013, it would have cost $72,000 per year. Our long-term care insurance policy would have covered that for about four years.

Prior to our visit, I talked on the phone with one of the administrators, the person who would be giving us a tour of the facility. I explained to her that Alan had signed legal papers requesting that if he ever had to live in a dementia facility, he wanted to be allowed to VSED when he could no longer feed himself. He just wanted the food to be placed nearby within reach of him. Although she said that the facility would cooperate and adhere to his Health Directive, she did not address VSED directly. When we were saying our good-byes, she hugged Alan, looked him in the eye, and said, "I hope I never see you here." This was remarkable because one of her tasks was to recruit people for the facility. Through my own research after Alan died, I learned that it's unlikely that any dementia facility will allow or assist with VSED, because they worry that there is too much legal liability. Perhaps this will change as VSED becomes more widely known and accepted.

We saw that the facility was attractive. The patients' rooms were adequate. The staff was pleasant. The patients were dressed and clean. The residents could walk outside into a garden area by themselves.

There are seven identifiable stages of Alzheimer's.

Ideally, this facility wanted residents to arrive during the fifth stage so they could become familiar with it before they lost their mental competency. However, we were told the majority moved in during the sixth or seventh stage. The day we toured the facility, we felt Alan had some symptoms from stage four and a few from stage five. The administrator proudly told us that their patients take an average of twelve medications a day, fewer than the average of seventeen medications given to patients in other facilities. Alan was taking only thyroid medication, and many supplements prescribed by his naturopath.

We saw two groups of patients. The first group represented the least advanced in terms of Alzheimer's. They were playing an indoor game of bowling. It was relatively quiet. One at a time, someone would get up and throw the bowling ball very slowly. Most of the others were slumped over in their chairs in a stupor and were not participating.

Next, we were ushered to a room where patients in the last stages of Alzheimer's were in a "music session." One woman was slumped over a table banging, over and over, loudly on a drum. All the other patients were slumped over in their chairs, a few of them obviously asleep. They all seemed heavily medicated. Alan and I stood in this room for no more than five minutes. We both became shaky. We clutched onto one another and left the room. We found a couch and sat down and cried together at what we had seen.

As soon as we left the facility, Alan turned to me and said, "I will never live there." This was such a sad day for us. We never discussed that option again.

Alan had made up his mind. He said he was going to VSED. I began, slowly, to accept and support his decision.

I experienced many emotions. I was relieved that he would not have to live into the late stages of Alzheimer's.

I knew it was more than I could handle to see him decline in a dementia facility. But I had already been grieving for about four years as I watched him decline, going from doctor to doctor. Now the grief moved to a deeper level.

I repeatedly asked Alan if he was certain that he truly wanted to VSED. I asked him so many times that he finally turned to me one day and said, "Please, don't ask me anymore. I've made up my mind. This is what I'm going to do."

Becoming Alan's Advocate and Manager

Now came the most difficult time I have ever experienced. I realized fully that making VSED happen for Alan was up to me. I didn't know anyone who had done this. I had no expert to approach and no guidebook to read. Alan and I had discussed everything *together* beforehand, and now he could no longer help me with the details and arrangements. I did tell him, however, step by step, everything I was doing. In addition, I had to take care of everything in our household by myself.

I felt flooded with questions. How could Alan VSED with dignity? Could we do this alone? What sort of help would we need? Would doctors support us? Even though this is legal, would people who don't know that try to stop us? How would I help Alan throughout the VSED process? Who would support and take care of me? All of these questions were overwhelming.

Everything in our lives was heightened, filled with meaning. We faced this time consciously, but each in our own way. We were both deeply alive, feeling every emotion. Alan's emotions moved through him easily. When he was sad, he was feeling the emotion of sadness, not self-pity. He was witnessing what was occurring at the moment. Then that feeling passed until another arose. He was freer than I was. Difficult emotions got hold of me, and would not leave.

Alan's short-term memory was becoming worse. He seemed unaware of the past. He had heightened awareness of the present moment, but would not stay with anything for long. He would be involved in something and then easily nod off and fall asleep. He never became angry. He was grateful to everyone who helped him. He was glad to still be alive.

During this time, I felt almost unbearable sadness and despair. I no longer laughed and had a difficult time enjoying myself. I experienced great waves of anxiety. I had trouble sleeping. I'd wake up multiple times in the middle of the night, and my first thought would be, "How is this going to resolve?" I began to see a therapist. Every week I witnessed my despair and sadness openly. Alan went with me a couple of times and alone several times. He continued to experience calm and equanimity. I didn't. Nevertheless, I had a strong emotional and physical constitution and every day I put one foot in front of the other and did what I felt I had to do so Alan could have his wish.

In Chapter Three, I will detail all the specific tasks I completed to prepare for Alan's VSED.

Alan Attended His Own Funeral

After Alan made the decision to stop eating and drinking, he still had some good living to experience. Although we knew it was essential that he determine markers or signs to help him set a date to start the VSED process, he still wanted to live as long and as fully as possible.

He used to laugh and think it was funny that people have funerals after they die! He thought it was sad that dead people have to miss all the love and attention showered on them at their funerals! We decided this did not need to be the case for him, and set about preparing his ceremony. We called the event his Celebration of Life and scheduled it at a time when he could still speak fairly well. He was very clear that he wanted to share thoughts and ideas with his friends and family.

About ninety people attended the event, held at our local Center for Spiritual Living. The band played beautiful music, and Alan requested some special songs be sung. I was sitting by his side and also spoke. His sister performed a beautiful hula in his honor. After a wonderful shared meal, it was time to leave. It was dark when we left the building, and all the attendees formed a long line behind us. Each person had a lit candle and they followed us to our car. We were surrounded by love.

Below is some of what Alan shared that night on October 20, 2012. He and I talked ahead of time about what he wanted to say. Then I wrote a script for him, and he read most of it at the Celebration. He improvised a little, too. By this time, Alan had made his decision and knew that he would experience VSED in the not too distant future. He was feeling joyous and peaceful and loved on this evening.

Alan: What I want to share with you is what I remember today. I used to be able to do a lot of things: use the computer, play music, teach Neuro-Linguistic Programming, help high school kids prepare for S. A. T. exams. They were all interesting and valuable. These are things that I can't do anymore.

I'm at peace with all of this. It doesn't upset me to sit at the computer and not be able to figure out how to do stuff. It used to upset me but it doesn't anymore. I just ask for help, and it's okay. It's almost a given that, especially guys, when they can't do their job, feel worthless. I don't feel that.

All the things that used to be important to my ego aren't important anymore. I can't play music anymore. I lose track, play the wrong things. And that's okay. It used to be important to me that I was the keyboard player at this Center. But that's not important now. Nothing feels particularly important. I don't have the words for it. I can still play the piano for myself and have as much pleasure as I used to.

A Celebration of Life used to be for people who are no longer here. I decided that if there was going to be a celebration of life for me, I wanted to be there for it.

If I were celebrating the life of Alan Alberts, I would remember that he was educated, very smart, always curious, experimented with different lifestyles and life experiences.

Music has been a life-long learning trip starting with the piano when I was six. I had a very strict piano teacher. I liked to stick in notes that weren't in the music. Every time I did that, she'd get pissed off. One time my mother brought me the sheet music for "Zippity Doo Dah." She said, "I was hoping it would motivate you to play more."

I went to my lesson. My piano teacher said, with disgust, "What is this?" I said, "It's a popular song." She said, "Well, play it." I said, "I can't. I didn't learn it." So she said, "You don't have to learn it, you just read the chords and play it."

She showed me how to sit down with a piece of music that was only melody and chords. She taught me a lot about chords. So I stopped taking lessons and started buying sheet music with chords.

In high school, I was at Andover Phillips Academy (John F. Kennedy went there before me, George Bush went there after me). I was in a dance band there, and the marching band, and played drums a little bit. I took at least one music course. At the end of four years I won a prize.

A guy who had been at Andover donated a bunch of money so the school could buy a set of carillon bells. He came back one day to a reunion and said, "Where are my bells?" They were in some basement. He paid to have a bell tower built. The school hung the bells but no one played them. When he came the next time, he gave another endowment, the interest of which was to provide a scholarship for someone to learn to play the bells. I don't remember how I got to be that person. But it was great with me because I had to play the bells during chapel and I didn't want to go to chapel. So I learned to play the carillon bells. They're not tuned very well. I'd just improvise. People would come up to me and say, "I loved that Bach cantata you played." I didn't tell them it was my improvisation of "Blue Moon."

My shirt is symbolic for me. (Alan was wearing a shirt with the Harvard logo on it.) My dad went to Harvard. My uncles went to Harvard. My cousins went. I thought Harvard was the best college, and I just assumed I was going. Not that they could get me in. I never thought about how hard it might be to get in. I wanted to go.

One time in the second grade, we took IQ tests. I got the highest score. I never before had thought of myself as smart. That stuck in my mind.

My high school guidance teacher said I would get in to Harvard and not to apply anywhere else. I think I took the first computer course ever given in the world at Harvard.

This year, 2,032 students were admitted, 5.9

percent of the applicant pool of 34,302. I didn't even think about this kind of thing at the time. It was the same when I went to graduate school. I decided I wanted to go to U.C. Berkeley. I knew it was a good school. They had a computer science department. It was in California. And there was this girl there, and it was as far away from my parents as I could get and still be in the United States.

So I packed up and moved to Berkeley. I went to the admissions office. Standing at a window, I said, "I'm Alan Alberts. I went to Harvard and I'd like to go to graduate school here." The woman at the window said, "Well, you'll have to apply." I said okay and asked for the application papers. This was 1962, I think. I just felt, "You guys should let me in."

It's a state of mind. Part of the Science of Mind philosophy is that you get what you believe, what you assume. That was true for me long before I ever heard of Science of Mind. It was a useful image to have for business.

I was always looking for something that had some meaning beyond what was in front of me. While at Harvard, I discovered Transcendental Meditation. While in graduate school at Berkeley, I joined a Gurdjieff group in the 1960s. Gurdjieff was a Russian Mystic. I can't tell you anything else about it. I have no memory of what we did. And that's okay.

Later I learned how to be an EMT. I did massage therapy, reflexology, Neuro-Linguistic Programming. I learned how to drive an ambulance, which was probably the most fun.

And I continued to learn more about music, about the piano, playing with famed jazz trombonist,

Frank Rehak. I had no idea at the time how famous he was, and I don't remember now. But it's okay. I lived in an intentional community for a while. One day, I was playing the piano. Frank Rehak came through and said, "We need a piano player for our band." So I went with him to meet the band. Frank said to the other musicians, "Why don't we start out with the blues. There are three chords for the blues, and everybody knows them. Well, I didn't know them, but I had them in my room. So I ran up and got them. The band players all said, "Who is this guy who doesn't know three blues chords?" But I played with Frank Rehak for about ten years, until he died from cancer. I learned a lot about music.

In my late forties, I became a paralegal and went to law school for a while. This led to the business that Phyllis and I developed: teaching lawyers how to use computers in their offices for everything from billing to case management. We gave a lot of seminars. Sometimes I'd bring a portable electronic piano with us to illustrate what computers could do. I would play a simple tune on the keyboard and then the keyboard's computer would play it back and I'd accompany it.

This is a Celebration of my life and what I have learned from living it. What I've learned is: It doesn't make much difference what you do. Your life is your life and then it's over. To be happy, do what you want to do. There is nothing to be afraid of when you're dying. Even though I don't know what's coming, that's okay. Sometime I'm going to realize that I'm not alive any more. I'm hoping I go someplace where I can realize that, but I may not.

Setting a Date to Begin VSED

The most frequent question I'm asked by others regarding Alan's VSED experience is, "How did he know when it was time to start?"

This *is* the critical question. Anyone who is thinking about VSED needs to determine a recognizable symptom, what we call a "marker," some action or event that signals, this is the time to set a date to begin. Our goal was for Alan to live as long as he could with some quality of life but not so long that he would no longer have the mental capacity to follow through with the VSED process.

In Alan's case, he made his decision to VSED six months before he actually started the process. However, once he made this decision, he kept changing his start date. This was one of the most difficult things for me to handle emotionally. Every time I would prepare myself for the date he chose, he would change it. Of course, I understood. I knew how difficult it was for him to decide.

Four months before he died, he said, "Regarding the quality of my life, as long as I can go to the Center for Spiritual Living and enjoy it, then I want to stay alive. When that changes, then it will be time for me to VSED. And, if I get an acute illness and I can't decide for myself, then let me die. If I can't have this kind of discussion about whether or not I should be treated, then let me die." These words were actually put in his Health Directive, a document I will discuss in the Appendix.

We had been attending our local Center for Spiritual Living for many years. As his Alzheimer's became worse, he had to stop playing in the band there, but he took this in his stride. This Center represented love and community for Alan and provided loving support for both of us throughout Alan's illnesses. One day, we went to the Center for what we realized would be our last time. It took all of Alan's energy to ride there, sit for an hour, and ride back home, less than two hours for the entire trip. Alan moved ever so slowly, and when we arrived back home, he was completely exhausted. We sat at our dining room table. Alan said, "I can't go to the Center anymore. I'm just too tired. It's time for me to start the VSED process." I told him I agreed with him. I looked at him and said, "It's hard for me that you keep changing the date. You asked me to tell you if I thought that you were getting close to the point of not being able to follow through with your decision because your mind was getting too foggy. I feel you are close to the point."

We continued our conversation. I said that I thought he would not be mentally competent in another two months, three at the most, and then he wouldn't be able to VSED because he wouldn't remember why he wasn't eating or drinking. I also told him that I was running out of energy and that after a couple more months, I would have to consider having him live in a facility. This conversation lasted about twenty minutes. He said he wanted to talk one more time with one of our counselors. I thought that was a good idea too and made an appointment for the next morning. We were both on that phone call with the counselor. When the call was over, he turned to me and said, "I'm starting in one week."

Later in the afternoon, I asked him how he was doing. He said with tears in his eyes, "I'm feeling sad." Later that evening, I asked him again. He said, "It's a done deal." That was the last time we talked about it. The date was set. I began to handle all the details for him to begin the VSED process.

Alan's Experience: Preparing to Die

Once he made his decision to VSED, Alan became increasingly comfortable and at peace with his decision and with himself. He said to several friends, "When I didn't know anything about this, it sounded horrible. Now that I've investigated it, it doesn't sound horrible at all, and I'm going to do it. I'm doing it because I have a disease that will rob me of the ability to make this choice. I have Alzheimer's, and Phyllis and I went to visit an Alzheimer's facility, and I couldn't imagine living there. This helped me make my decision to VSED."

Now, Alan lived in a state of deep, calm, accepting presence. He spoke these actual words to me: "I am comfortable and at ease with everything. I just feel great all the time, even when I'm tired. I'm present all the time. I'm happy all the time. I didn't feel this way most of my life. People notice how happy I look. I think that's important because I'm really at the end of this life. Before, I always felt burdened by all the things that I thought I should be doing, and I'm not worried about that anymore. I have no fear of dying. I'm sure there are more exciting things that will happen to me. If you can will yourself to die, then you can." Alan was in a state of complete acceptance. He was not attached to anything, including me.

Alan also said this to me, with tears in his eyes: "I'm not sure how to share this calm I feel with other people. I think it's up to you, Phyllis, to share this with others. I'd love to help people reduce their suffering."

As many people do, Alan did have some "unfinished business" that he was now highly motivated to complete. In his case, his deep sadness revolved around his mother. He decided to work with a hypnotherapist who was also familiar with Neuro-Linguistic Programming. The therapist set up a session as though his mother were in the room with him, and together they provided her with resources she hadn't had when he was young, like the ability to be empathic, conscious, and self-loving. With her in that state, Alan was able to express to her the pain he had lived with his whole life: his belief that his mother didn't love him. Alan was able to see that her criticism of him was an expression of her own unmet needs, her craving for love and personal power. In this "movie," she could truly hear him, ask for forgiveness, and tell him how much she loved him. The heaviness in his heart was released by his tears and willingness to receive her love. This healing was profound for him. Perhaps Alan could have completed this work earlier, but his impending death motivated him to do the work now.

In the weeks prior to Alan's starting the VSED process, we had frequent brief conversations. I asked him: "How does this feel to you to make this decision, to anticipate this big shift? I found it fascinating that Alan compared starting VSED with other major moves in his life. "It feels like it did when I moved to Andover to start high school; when I moved to Cambridge to start college; when I moved into community; when I moved to Bellingham—like new worlds to learn about, new things to do. I looked toward all those things with eagerness."

Another time he volunteered this: "Dying is the unknown. It is like going to a new summer camp. You don't know what you'll be doing, who your friends will be. I'm just apprehensive about moving to a new place and it's an unknown. Will I know anybody there? Will I be conscious? I don't have fear, just a little apprehension."

We made an appointment with the chaplain at End of Life Washington who spent about two hours with us. She asked Alan about his end of life wishes. Did he want to leave a written or spoken legacy for his grandchildren? What specific people did he want to have in the house while he was going through the VSED experience? What kind of music did he want to hear throughout the process? Did he have anything left that he wanted to do? This was a relaxed and poignant conversation among the three of us.

People who know ahead of time that they are going to

die have the option of making it a conscious experience. The way you live your life has everything to do with the way you choose to die. Some people fight and resist it. Some are able to move gracefully into acceptance and to be mindful about how the process of death occurs. Everyone's experience is different. Everyone's death is unique.

I'm glad I had the presence of mind to write down many of the comments Alan made during his last months, and I recommend this idea to others. I treasure those notes now. His words are part of the legacy he left for all of us.

Alan once told me, "I'm thinking through a dirty screen." Yet he was able to communicate about the profound process he was involved in, preparing himself to set a date and have a conscious, elective death. He was quite aware that he could no longer concentrate well or do very much for himself. Nevertheless, the last six months of his life were precious and meaningful to him. He frequently felt sad, but did not feel self-pity. He was not able to track much of what was going on, but was quite present to what he was *feeling* in the moment.

What follows are some of the comments he made during our conversations in the last months of his life. I am quoting his exact words.

> "The parts of my brain that have changed have to do with the monkey chatter. My mind is quieter now."

> "This may be the best time in my life. I have no worries. There is nothing that I'm supposed to do anymore. I don't have any practical concerns. I'm not trying to accomplish anything. I have no cares. All this brings me peace. Like now, my computer doesn't work very well, and I don't care. I'd like it to work better, but I don't feel drawn to fixing it

myself. There are a lot of things I did five years ago that I just can't do now, and it's okay. I enjoy each day. There is less obligation, fewer expectations of me. I'd prefer to be the way I was, but I'm not. And that's okay."

"As each minute passes, whatever I'm doing is what I'm doing, and I don't wish I were doing something else, as I did when I was younger. Before, I used to wish I were doing something else. No matter what I was doing, there were other things I *could* be doing, *should* be doing, and that's all gone."

"My life is very good. People come and feed me, rub me, keep me company, laugh with me, especially the caregivers."

"People who have passed over are waiting for me. It is a living moving picture, not a static picture. I think my family is waiting for me: my mother, father, aunts and uncles. I'd like to see my piano teacher and be able to thank her for teaching me how to read sheet music."

"I would like to stay here until my next birthday, May 20, 2013. After that, it will be a good time to go." Alan said all this with certainty and enthusiasm, so I asked him, "Are you beginning to look forward to what comes next more than what you have now?" He said, "Yes."

"I feel happy today. I haven't said that in a very long time."

"Whatever is happening now is okay. Not
knowing how this will resolve is okay. Knowing
I will die soon is okay. I have no idea why I am so
accepting now. It just is. I wasn't always this way."

I recall one experience that seemed to be a marker for us,
that made us very sad. I was walking down the stairs inside
our house. For a moment, Alan thought he was in the house
where he was raised and that it was his mother who was
coming down the stairs. This is the first time something like
this happened. We held each other and cried.

Our conversations continued over Alan's last months.
We didn't talk a lot to one another. There wasn't much to
say anymore. We hugged a lot, and occasionally I asked
him questions. I asked, "Is there anything you're pissed
off at now?" He said, "No." I asked, "Do you feel there
are any things you need to resolve in your life?" He said,
"No." I asked, "Is there anything you still need to do?"
He said, "No." I asked, "Do you think about the future
much? Do you worry about it?" Alan said, "No. I don't
think about it much and I don't worry about it. Now I am
present. I don't think about the future or the past."

There was some levity during this time, too. During his
last months, Alan spent a lot of time in bed. I walked into
his bedroom one evening and he was watching Seinfeld
reruns on a small portable DVD player. His daughter
had sent him the Seinfeld reruns. I asked him, "Do you
want me to ask your daughter to send more DVDs?" Alan
replied, "No, wait until I watch these and then I can thank
her." I responded, "One of the good things about having
Alzheimer's is that you can watch them all, and then just
watch them all over again… Oh I'm sorry. It wasn't very
nice for me to make an Alzheimer's joke." Alan replied
thoughtfully, "What? I forgot already." Alan knew that
this was funny.

Another wonderful part of Alan's last few months is that he thoroughly enjoyed eating whatever he wanted. For health reasons, especially when we were curing his cancer, we usually adhered to a strict diet. Finally, one day Alan turned to me and said, "I'm eating whatever I want." After that, he thoroughly enjoyed eating ice cream and cookies, and anything else that he wanted, with great delight.

I had my last substantive conversation with Alan four months before he died. I have included it in the Appendix. After that, he spoke more simply and with fewer words. He kept talking, though less and less, until the end.

For the last months of Alan's life, our caregivers left the house about 5:00 p.m. Then, often, very slowly and carefully, Alan would walk upstairs and spend a couple of hours in our special room that had a comfortable couch in it. It is where I do my writing, where I meditate and do yoga, and where I look at the beautiful Pacific Northwest sunsets. Peace is in this room. This is where we spent our last precious times together, sharing only a few words. We had already said what we needed to say to one another through our rich life together. Now we sat more in silence, holding one another, often shedding and sharing our tears of love and sadness.

CHAPTER THREE
My Experience as a VSED Advocate

Commitment, Acceptance, and Stress

There are two parts to my experience as the advocate for Alan as he confronted his Alzheimer's diagnosis and made his decision to VSED: my inner life and my outer life. I will talk first about my emotional journey, and then about the medical, legal, and logistical matters I had to manage, forging my way through unknown territory, since few guidelines existed. I feel happy that I am able to provide guidelines and information now, for others.

Nothing in my life prepared me for the emotional experience in which I found myself, once our story began to unfold. I had watched my mother take care of my father for many years through various diseases, including Alzheimer's. I didn't want that to be my fate.

Early in my relationship with Alan, I told him that I wouldn't take care of him when he grew older unless he took very good care of himself beforehand. I feel embarrassed to reveal this now, but that felt true for me at the time. I wanted to control Alan's destiny, his life journey. Years later, I learned that my declaration had hurt Alan's feelings deeply, and I apologized to him. Even then, I did not realize that my worst fear would eventually become a reality. And it had nothing to do with how well Alan took care of himself! Life happens. Letting go, and letting life unfold without trying to control it, has been one of the biggest emotional lessons for me.

Over the years, when we were with friends, Alan and I sometimes talked about this philosophical question: What is the responsibility of a human being to his or her partner? Are we ethically responsible to take care of our partners, in health and in sickness? I remember a conversation with my daughter and her friend when they were in their thirties in which they said they would not take care of their husbands through serious illness. They couldn't imagine devoting that much of their energy and life to this effort. Ahh, the naiveté of youth!

I now realize why wedding vows always say something like, "in sickness and in health." And I now know that it was not obligation or some philosophical principle that led me to devote myself to taking care of Alan. It was love.

I believe each of us has to answer this question for ourselves: What is right for me in this situation? What do I need to do to live within my own guidelines of integrity? We act in ways that are right for us at the time because it is rightful action. Alan was an integral part of my life journey. We took care of one another, and I was going to take care of him for the rest of his life.

Alan witnessed my sadness and despair, but he had great inner wisdom and knew instinctively that I would have to work it out for myself. He was not responsible for my emotional journey, and I was not responsible for his. We could certainly be there for each other, but we could not do each other's inner work.

This is one of the gifts I've received from being Alan's advocate and main caregiver. My life journey is learning what I need to do for my well-being and highest good. I chose to be Alan's caregiver and to do whatever was required of me throughout his illnesses and death. No one else manipulated me to do this, including Alan.

Throughout the activities and the months and years I will describe below, I felt vulnerable much of the time. Day after day, I was overwhelmed with grief, anxiety, and fear. I felt so sad that I was losing my best friend and husband, and I was also afraid, anticipating my future alone without him. My grief was complicated by the fact that we both had minimal guidance about how to go through the VSED process. I was figuring it all out as I went along. Perhaps worst of all was experiencing judgment based on other people's beliefs, something I will discuss in detail later. Feeling judged left me traumatized on some occasions, with acute stress. If VSED had already been an acceptable and known option in our culture, I believe I would have experienced less trauma.

On the other hand, I was warmed by the love and support of others. I experienced generosity and thoughtfulness beyond anything I had ever known. I now know that I was growing all the time. I was learning that I could rely on my own resourcefulness. I saw that the only way out of grief was to go through it and experience it, that there were no short cuts. I gradually saw that my fears could not stop me from doing what I had to do, and that heartbreak is endurable in the end. These are powerful lessons.

I maintained my practice of yoga, meditation, and daily walks, and reached out to friends when I needed support. I sought professional help, which served to anchor me and keep me going in a straight line. I think what sustained me most was my focus on the tasks at hand, paying attention to Alan and his needs, doing all that needed to be done. I was busy. As an advocate and manager, I had a job to do.

Job Description for a Caregiver

The role and responsibility of an advocate is immense,

and is constantly changing. In my case, because I lived with Alan, I became his case manager, nurse, cook, driver, coordinator of care, and liaison with doctors and specialists. I was involved with Alan's physical, emotional, and spiritual life. It is an all-encompassing job with never a day off emotionally. I had help from hired caregivers, so I had occasional time for my own self-care and diversion. But even then, my concerns for Alan were always foremost in my mind.

Hiring Caregivers to Assist

It was after Alan made his decision to VSED that I realized that we needed caregiving help in our house. I wasn't comfortable leaving Alan alone because his Alzheimer's was progressing. I contacted a local non-profit agency, the Northwest Regional Council, which offered part-time professional caregivers, free to people who qualified. It was a way to support unpaid family members who were providing care. According to them, it is estimated that family and friends are the sole source of assistance for nearly seventy-five percent of our nation's impaired seniors.

These caregivers came into our home twice per week for three hours each time. They were willing to do whatever I asked. They would clean, cook, visit with Alan, or stay with him so I could leave the house.

This respite care was a big help, and I soon realized I needed much more help than six hours a week. I began to interview potential candidates, whom I found mostly by word of mouth. Although I could have called a caregiving agency, it was important for me to interview people myself. It also was a little less expensive this way. They needed to be flexible and caring people, willing to help with cooking, household chores, and taking Alan for outings. By the time I hired these additional caregivers, I had already been taking care of Alan for several years, and I was worn out physically and emotionally.

When I hired caregivers initially, I relied on my intuition. It was essential that I liked them as people and felt they were conscientious and capable. All the people I interviewed had been trained as Certified Nursing Assistants. I asked about their experience. I wanted to know how they would treat Alan. Would they respect him and help him to be independent for as long as possible? I needed to know if they were kind and empathetic. They needed to be comfortable with my telling them what to do. Were they flexible and able to make changes readily? How good were their communication skills? Were they comfortable giving medications? Would they take Alan on outings for an hour or two? Would they cook for both Alan and me based on the recipes I gave them? Would they keep Alan's room clean and do minimal housekeeping? Bottom line, I needed to trust and like them. They were going to be in our house much of the time.

As a result of my interviews, I assembled a nice team, and one woman headed up the team so I didn't have to deal with the details of caregivers' schedules. The caregivers were hired in November of 2012, five months before Alan began to VSED.

Now we were confronted with a new challenge we had not anticipated: It was a huge invasion of our privacy to have caregivers in our home. Alan and I decided to be open with our conversations. We didn't keep our voices extra low so others couldn't hear us talk. We both understood that our demonstration was paving the way for other people in the future. This meant that the caregivers heard that Alan kept changing the date about when he was going to start VSED. They witnessed how everything affected me. They saw me crying. They became annoyed with me, and sometimes I would flare up at them. It was real life!

We traded our privacy for help and support. Caregivers are people with their own needs. Often they needed too much from me in terms of conversation. Because of the way our house is arranged physically, they were always visible. I valued them tremendously, but I wanted more privacy too. It was an ongoing conflict for me.

A Word About Long Term Care Insurance

When I was ready to hire caregivers beyond what the local agency provided at no cost, I contacted our Long-Term Care Insurance provider and opened our case, requesting that the insurance company cover the cost of my hiring caregivers. To my dismay, I had forgotten that the policy carries a ninety-day deductible period. I should have opened the case earlier and hired someone at least a couple of hours once a week in order to complete the deductible requirement. Dealing with these insurance bureaucrats was one of the most challenging and frustrating experiences of my whole story. After many difficult phone sessions, including one in which I lost my composure and yelled at the agent, "What would you do if this were your mother?" the insurance company finally agreed to accept the work that the agency caregivers did for us as the deductible—even though those caregivers were being paid by Northwest Regional Council and not me.

Farewell Visits

Another way we prepared for Alan's VSED process was to invite people to visit for several months before he began his fast. Friends and family came from afar and spent time with us. We talked openly about Alan's plan to VSED. It was always a tearful departure when people left. Friends seemed to be more shaken than Alan.

A few weeks before he set his final date, Alan said to me, "Please call my daughter and ask her to come and visit right away." I did this even though she had visited one month earlier. She was hesitant to come again so soon until I said, "If you wait, your dad may not be here in another three weeks." She arrived that weekend. Alan was in the process of letting go of his attachments to things and people. It was much more difficult for his daughter to let go of her dad, her stable rock.

Legal Support

Even though I had read that VSED is a legal option, I wanted to be absolutely certain that there would be no liability for anyone. I found an elder care attorney who helped us prepare several legal documents, which I have included in the Appendix. Even though these documents may not be strictly necessary in every case, I highly recommend them for everyone's comfort and security. As it turned out, I was called upon to produce them in one incident, which I will relate in Chapter Four.

The most important of the legal documents is a Health Directive. If you don't have this legal document that clearly appoints agents to act on your behalf and make healthcare decisions for you when you are incapable of doing so yourself, you will be turning over your power to doctors who don't know anything about you, and a hospital that may care more about their rules than about compassion in any given situation. It is my hope that someday, a Health Directive will become as routine for everyone as a driver's license. I have provided clear guidelines for preparing a health directive in the Appendix.

Assessing Mental Capacity

Throughout our elder care attorney's relationship with Alan, she informally assessed his level of mental capacity at each visit. She would ask him questions and be sure he had a clear understanding about his decision to VSED. She asked him what would happen if he changed his mind. He understood that his Alzheimer's would progress and that he would end up living in a dementia facility. In every conversation, he had clear understanding about what he was doing and what the consequences were. These conversations were necessary because our lawyer needed to be convinced that Alan was capable of understanding and signing legal documents.

Alan's doctor was also confident he had decision-making capacity. We were comfortable with these assessments by our attorney and doctor.

One result of the first national conference on VSED at Seattle University in October 2016, which I helped organize, was our realization that guidelines need to be developed to determine the mental capacity of a person who elects to do VSED, especially for people in the early stages of Alzheimer's and other neurological diseases. From a technical perspective, legal competence is not the same as medical capacity. Doctors and lawyers view these situations differently.

Who should assess a person's mental capacity and competence to make a decision to VSED? Does a psychiatrist need to be involved? A chosen psychiatrist may not have had previous experience with the patient, and many psychiatrists are not experienced working with patients who are facing end of life decisions. The medical profession needs to address this question. Should there be different standards for a home setting and a clinical setting such as hospice? Timing is critical, because it is essential that the person who is going to VSED has the capacity to remember why he or she is not eating or drinking.

The Final Stages of Preparation
Five months after the caregivers started helping us, Alan became clear about when he was going to start the VSED

process, and I needed to arrange special support for his end of life process.

To start with, we would need twenty-four-hour support, so I began the interview process again. My criteria were different when I began to interview caregivers specifically for the VSED process. Many of the caregivers I interviewed were not comfortable with Alan's decision to VSED. Caregivers are trained to help people have a good quality of life for as long as possible, not to shorten their life with a good quality of death.

I first interviewed people whose specialty was taking care of people during the dying process. How much experience did they have taking care of people in their last days? What was their opinion about VSED? Could they support Alan throughout the process, including the last days of his life when he was comatose and couldn't move at all? Did they know what supplies were needed for end-of-life care? Could they follow doctor's orders? Were they comfortable administering narcotic medication? Could they be steady emotionally, even if I wasn't? The list of questions felt endless.

As we were approaching the date, one of the regular caregivers mentioned on a couple of occasions that everything would go well as long as I wasn't anxious. But I was extremely anxious, and it only increased my anxiety to have her criticizing me about it. This same caregiver, who was a true professional in her work, also didn't understand my request that I be the only person who could talk with Alan during the VSED process if he asked for food or water. She felt she was the professional and should be able to handle this herself.

I was uncomfortable having this caregiver in the house while Alan was going through the VSED process. I discussed this with a close friend who was a retired caregiver. She agreed that I needed to have people who were completely comfortable with both Alan and me. Three days before our start date, I fired the caregiver, even though she was competent in her work. This was difficult for me, but I felt I had made the right choice. Like an angel, my good friend with extensive caregiving experience stepped forward and became one of two caregivers to take care of Alan during the VSED experience. With them in place, and our doctor, we had an excellent team.

Supplies

As our start date grew closer, our caregivers gathered supplies that we would need in the house. I have listed them in the Appendix.

Medical Supervision

Good medical support is critical for a positive, comfortable VSED death. Hospice is set up to provide palliative and end-of-life care for dying patients, and hospice doctors are skilled at doing this. However, in our case, our local hospice turned out to be unavailable for Alan. They said they would not help him until he was in the end stage of coma, and I knew that he might have endured deep suffering if he didn't have proper medical support throughout his VSED process. I know of other people, in the larger Seattle area, whom hospice did support through the VSED process. In the two cases I know of, hospice accepted the person on the second day of the fast.

We had known our doctor for several years, and we adored her. She had mentioned to Alan that she would take care of him for the rest of his days. When hospice refused to help us, I called her. I never even had to ask her to step in and help. Upon hearing hospice's decision, she immediately said, "Then I'm going to come forward and take care of Alan." It felt like she was another angel in disguise coming to our rescue. She made three house calls during the nine and a half days, and she was available twenty-four hours each day by phone. There were times when we called her in the middle of the night.

Once the VSED process started, Alan knew he had a choice about whether or not he wanted medication. Yet he told our doctor that he wanted as little medication as possible because he wanted to be as conscious as possible throughout the process. Our good doctor stayed one step ahead of him and made sure he was comfortable. I didn't want him to suffer at all. The amount of medication a person receives is personal and will depend on the patient-doctor relationship and circumstances.

Managing the Opinions of Others

Because Alan and I were not secretive about what we were doing, everyone had an opinion about it, and they all felt a need to express theirs with me! With all the details I was managing, on top of my own emotional journey, coping with the rest of the world's need to express their judgments added to my stress.

Most people were surprised and curious, having never heard of VSED as an end-of-life option. They had questions and uncertainties. Our clarity helped many people to embrace our choice along with us. But there were others who, we knew, were critical. They would have made a different choice for themselves and needed to be sure we knew how they felt. It was very difficult for me to have my husband die, and at the same time not receive support from certain friends.

For example, one friend called me two days before Alan's start date and began to question me. I felt angry, but still explained that Alan's choice and my support came from a deep place of love between us. I then asked her not to come around our house if she could not support us. About the same time, another friend arrived at our house, uninvited, and began to ask Alan if she should research cures for Alzheimer's. I realized I did not need to, nor could I, justify our choice to her, and I asked her to leave.

What hurt most of all was the undercurrent of opinion that I was pressuring Alan to VSED, or that he was doing it as a favor to me. One of the caregivers who had been helping us for five months did not like this gossip either. Here is how she handled it.

Four or five weeks before Alan started VSED, I heard other caregivers not trusting Phyllis' motives, and I too became unsure. One of them tried to convince me that Phyllis was persuading Alan to die because she was so stressed and tired. So I decided to speak with Alan personally. One morning, after I made Alan's breakfast, I sat down with him. I asked him if he was comfortable with VSED. He said, "Yes, very comfortable." (Alan is a man of few words, even without Alzheimer's.) I said there was talk going around that Phyllis was pressuring him to VSED. Without hesitation, Alan said, "Phyllis has been working for a long time to take care of me. I love her and trust her. It's because of Phyllis that I feel comfortable doing this. I am ready." I can recall even now his peaceful face and the energy in his voice. I knew in my heart that as an evolved being he knew exactly what was going on around him, and he knew exactly what he was doing. After this conversation, I felt peace in my heart, and from that point on, I was in support of his decision and committed to doing whatever it took to keep him comfortable. I felt honored to have known him. I wish I had known him before. I always left their house feeling more balanced.

Alan had been admitted to our local hospice service three months earlier for "failure to thrive." We adored everyone associated with them, felt grateful, and had a most positive experience. Alan was released from hospice when they felt he was not in the last six months of life; however, they said they would be available when Alan made the decision to VSED. It was a great shock and terribly sad for me when they told me they would not help Alan at the end of his life until he was in the end stage of coma. I had been counting on their support and felt like the foundation under me cracked. Our hospice is owned by the Catholic Church, and it is my understanding that they do not "believe" in VSED.

One of Alan's favorite quotes, and a guideline for how he lived his life, is this: "A belief is just a story that you tell yourself about what is. A belief is just a feeling of certainty about what is. A belief is not the truth."

In the end, there is very little essential "Truth." Most of what we think or believe is based on stories we have been told or that we tell ourselves, or individual perceptions, not essential Truth. We were not concerned with how someone labeled Alan's choice. This labeling was based on that person's subjective beliefs, stories, and imprinting. Their "belief" wasn't an issue for us. What was upsetting for us was when they verbalized and acted out their beliefs around us, as did hospice, certain friends, some of the caregivers. They thought their beliefs were the Truth and they wanted us to behave in accord with their "beliefs" instead of our own. Beliefs are personal; they are arbitrary. Our "belief" centered on doing the most loving action possible in any situation, including this one, and that is what we were doing. In the end, most of what we say and live by are beliefs, not the absolute Truth. Truth is indisputable; beliefs shift and change.

After Alan died and while I was preparing my TEDx talk, I asked many people how Alan's demonstration affected them. Most comments were overwhelmingly positive and reveal the beneficial impact that our experience had on so many people.

"I feel hopeful that we might all maintain our integrity and power to the very end as Alan did."

"It was one of the most loving, beautiful, and heroic deaths I have ever witnessed."

"I feel happy for Alan that he avoided the dread of descending into Alzheimer's."

"I'm grateful for his public, courageous demonstration of his civil rights at the end of his life."

"He and every human being deserve to choose their passing."

"You gave him an enormous gift to help him pass with compassion."

"His final days will always be an inspiration to me."

"My dear friend, Alan, showed me something I never thought about before. Through his conscious decision and clear action to VSED, I realize that I too can make such a choice. This awareness gives me immeasurable relief and peace."

"Your clarity and focus to VSED teaches me much more than words about how to live and die."

"I am an experienced private caregiver and have witnessed the debilitating stages of Alzheimer's and Parkinson's disease. You have courageously paved the way for others to also have a conscious choice about how they leave this world, affording them the opportunity to tie loose ends, forgive and heal relationships and themselves, and leave this world with peace of mind, heart, and soul. This option is desperately needed.

"I was deeply moved to see Alan embrace death,

rather than reject life. He was so peaceful and clear."

"At a time when many endure prolonged Alzheimer's suffering, Alan died a planned and peaceful death with VSED. It was one of the most loving, beautiful, and heroic deaths I have ever witnessed."

"VSED is consciously releasing life within a supportive loving and living embrace."

CHAPTER FOUR
What Happened During the Fast:
Alan's Last Nine and a Half Days

My Account of the Final Days

After Alan's last conversation with his counselor, he decided to start the VSED process on April 10, 2013. At last, that long anticipated day arrived. We were there.

Anticipating what my own experience would be and what I would need, I invited a friend to stay with me for the duration of the fast. Her job would be to take care of my emotional needs throughout the process. This worked well for me, and is something I recommend to others. Emotional support for the advocate is a critically important component of the overall planning.

On the morning the fast began, a spiritual friend came to bless our house. We set up a beautiful altar with memorabilia from Alan's life and kept twenty-four-hour candles burning throughout the process, representing the beauty and light of Alan as a human being. Having these symbols was not important to Alan, but it meant the world to me. When I solicited Alan's opinion about what should happen after he died, for example, where I should put his ashes, he always responded in the same way. "I don't care. Do whatever you like. I'm not going to be here!"

A volunteer doctor at End of Life Washington had told us what the fast could be like for Alan, and what we might expect. Initially, he said, Alan would experience hunger and then thirst. The hunger would diminish after two or three days, but his mouth would be dry, and this could be powerfully uncomfortable. We would need to keep his mouth moist. Also, Alan would need medication to stay comfortable, most likely morphine and lorazepam. He assured us that any competent doctor would know what to do and emphasized the importance of engaging one who would be willing to make regular visits and to be available on the phone twenty-four hours a day. It would be critical that Alan stay comfortable and out of pain. If Alan became ill with any acute illness before he started the VSED process, we should keep Alan comfortable and let the illness take its toll.

This same doctor also suggested that Alan reduce his intake to five hundred calories a day for five days prior to starting the VSED process. Alan had excellent self-control and determination, and was able to do this. He ate an egg or two at breakfast, and a snack in the evening. His last meal was at 6:00 p.m. when he ate two small scoops of vanilla ice cream.

Two nights before Alan began, I helped him find the words to set his intention. "I think within one week I will die. It will be easy and I will be free of suffering."

On our last evening together, before this sacred and courageous process began, I went into Alan's bedroom and sat on his double bed. The bed was high because there were drawers all around the bottom of it where many of Alan's clothes were kept. I had to empty the drawers because the next morning that bed would be taken away so that a hospital bed could be delivered.

Systematically, I began to empty one drawer at a time and make piles of clothes. Then I began to put them into boxes. I knew I would be giving his clothes away soon after he died. Alan watched with little emotion. As we talked about what I was doing, and what I would do with his clothes, the whole experience felt completely surreal to me. Suddenly, we both broke out into hysterical laughter. It was the last time we laughed together. Deep laughter was one of the things I cherished the most about my relationship with my husband. We laughed as we had not done in a long time, not through his illnesses. The laughter felt so good. Alan was free and ready.

Before I went to bed that night, I cleaned the kitchen and put all visible food away. I knew I could not have any food odors in the house during the VSED process.

All of Alan's needs were met by me, our doctor, and two caregivers who each worked a twelve-hour shift per day. The doctor, by now a friend of ours, came to our house three times during the VSED process, and made herself available to us by phone twenty-four hours per day. There were times we called her in the middle of the night. Her personal account of the experience is included below. Also, our primary caregiver has provided a detailed, day-by-day account of Alan's physical experience and his medical and care interventions at the end of this chapter, for anyone interested in specific details.

On the first official day of Alan's fast, I went into his bedroom about 8:00 a.m. I've heard of people going through VSED and holding court with others, getting out of bed, going for walks during the early days. It was different for Alan. He basically went to bed and stopped eating and drinking. He was finished with living, and now he was allowing himself to die so he didn't have to live into the late stages of Alzheimer's. He was certain he wanted to do this, and he knew why. He had prepared himself well.

What happened next surprised us. Rather suddenly, Alan

became more alert and had more energy. It was puzzling to us to see him become more active just when we thought he would be losing energy. He seemed almost euphoric and began talking about how curious he was about what may come next after he died.

What no one had prepared us for was that reduced calories would put Alan into ketosis, which causes a more alert state. Ketosis happens when the body is not receiving enough food to supply energy and begins trying to obtain it by breaking down body fat. Ketones are fuel, and they burn more efficiently than glucose. It was as if his brain was receiving super food, but this was sustained for only a short period of time. While he was in ketosis, Alan also slept less.

In the first days, Alan still turned to the habitual process that had been part of his waking routine for months. For instance, he kept picking up the *New Yorker* magazine and appeared to be reading it. It was doubtful that he was. He continued to listen to NPR on the radio. He had a miniature DVD player and he continued to watch the same Seinfeld shows over and over.

Alan did still want to get out of bed to use the bathroom, and he had a hard time doing this. One of my biggest sources of anxiety for the months we were preparing for the VSED process was that Alan would fall and end up in the hospital. Such an occurrence would almost certainly have derailed his plan. His doctor said that the medication he would need in the hospital (and possibly a nursing home afterward) would bring on "sundowning syndrome," with increased agitation and confusion most of the time. Alan would lose his orientation to place, time, and person, and would no longer be sufficiently competent to VSED. To prevent any such accident, we were very concerned that Alan have assistance whenever he got out of bed. He was not very steady on his feet by this time.

On Friday, April 12, day three of the fast, a most

surprising—indeed shocking—event occurred. Apparently, someone had called Adult Protective Services. We received a call from a social worker announcing that someone had called to report possible elder abuse and that she would be at our house in ten minutes to investigate.

I was stunned! But I'm glad I didn't have more notice because it would only have given me more time to become upset.

When the social worker arrived, I took her into the living room where we had the altar set up, and answered some preliminary questions. I let Alan know that she was at the house and why she had come. It felt surreal that this was happening. There was so much love in our house, and we were being investigated for abuse!

The social worker and I went into Alan's bedroom and sat at the foot of his bed. She began to ask him questions, and he was able to answer all of them. I left them alone for a few minutes and went upstairs to call our elder care attorney and gather all of our legal documents together. I felt composed and prepared. It felt like another energy slipped into my body and put me into a relaxed state. I walked back downstairs and slipped my arm through the arm of the social worker and calmly said, "Come with me into my classroom. I'm going to educate you about Voluntarily Stopping Eating and Drinking." I led her into the kitchen area where we could sit together at the dining room table. Systematically, I showed her one document after another. She wrote fast and took copious notes. I showed her Alan's Health Directive, his Alzheimer's Advance Mental Health Directive, the long white paper by Thaddeus Pope and Lindsey Anderson that described VSED as a legal option. I also showed her the witnessed and notarized Release and Assumption of Risk statements. Alan had signed one over his name, and I did the same over my name on a separate document. This last document protected the doctor, caregivers, and myself, clearly showing that Alan took all the responsibility for his decision. I told her that the U.S Supreme Court in 1997 confirmed that anyone may refuse lifesaving medical treatment, including food and hydration.

One week later I learned that the social worker wrote a positive report and that the case was closed and could not be reopened. Later I received a letter from her. She wrote, "I'm glad to have met you, and I truly appreciate all I learned from you. Your courage, strength, and love were and are unique to behold."

Our doctor had told me that on several of Alan's office visits to see her, he had asked her questions about VSED. On one of those visits, Alan said that if he decided to VSED, he wanted to be sedated to comfort right from the beginning of the process. So Dr. Dora was surprised when she met with Alan on the first day of his VSED experience when he told her that he wanted as little medication as possible because he wanted to be as conscious as possible throughout the process. As mentioned, our doctor stayed one step ahead of him and made sure he was comfortable.

We continued to keep Alan comfortable. We played the music he had selected ahead of time. We had a humidifier in the room, and we moistened his mouth regularly. We massaged his body gently with lotion and turned him in bed regularly to prevent bedsores. Our caregivers were both Certified Nursing Assistants and were well trained. One of them had also been taking care of Alan for the previous five months. I was clear that I wanted to be present throughout the entire process, but I was also clear that I did not want to do the physical caregiving. These are very personal decisions.

For the first couple of days, Alan wanted to spend much of the time alone in his room. He had already said goodbye to everyone. Friends and family had been visiting for some months. Each day, his daughter called in the evening, and we put the speaker phone to his ear so he could hear her loving words.

Every day Alan became visibly weaker and wobblier. After two days, he couldn't get out of bed by himself without assistance. He went from being able to toilet himself, to using the commode, then the urinal and then had a diaper placed on him. He was frequently turned in bed when he couldn't do this himself.

On days three and four, Alan had some increased restlessness and showed some signs of discomfort due to dehydration. He never complained about hunger. Whenever he showed any signs of discomfort, he was given appropriate medication, as prescribed by our doctor. If a physician has legitimately ordered medication, the patient may self-administer it. If the patient needs help or is sedated, someone else may administer the medication. In our situation, most of the medication was given by the caregivers, and occasionally by me.

By the fourth day, Alan wanted people around him more, and he wanted to be touched gently. One of the caregivers knew how to do some Jin Shin Jyutsu. She showed us what to do, and we did this on Alan for the rest of his VSED journey. Simply, Jin Shin Jyutsu helps to release tension in the body. I happen to also be trained in Reiki and Therapeutic Touch, which I used on the last day of his life.

I gave the caregivers explicit instructions that I be the only person who could talk with Alan if he asked for food or water. I had anticipated this possibility and had given much thought to it. Of course I was prepared to give him anything he requested. It would have been cruel and illegal for me not to.

On two occasions, on the fourth and fifth days, he did ask me for water. This is what I said to him: "You said you want to die so you don't have to live into the late stages of Alzheimer's. I'm happy to give you water, but I want you to know that it will extend the amount of time it takes you to die. Would you like a glass of water, or would it be enough for me spray mists of water into your mouth until you are satisfied?" He understood my words and said the mists of water would be enough. I sprayed and sprayed, and he lapped up the water like a kitty. He seemed satisfied and did not request water again. This is why mental competency is important throughout the VSED process. Alan had to be aware of what was happening, and why.

As each day passed, I began to spend more and more time with Alan in his room. Being together in this way was comforting to both of us. On the sixth day, I began to spend much of my time actually in bed with Alan, in his small hospital bed. On this day, he could only talk metaphorically. Also on this day, he looked at his imaginary watch, and said, "I've got to get the milk. What time is it? The people are at the party." This sounds very similar to words that I've read in other books about end of life occurrences. It seemed that Alan was already living—or dying—into a new experience that was very real to him.

On the eighth day, we could hear the rattling in Alan's lungs. He was kept comfortable with medication. He could no longer communicate with his words, and his eyes were now permanently closed. I got close to him and said, "Alan, I am here with you. If you are comfortable, blink your eyes." With his eyes still closed, he was able to move them. I could see the movement under his eyelids, and I knew he was comfortable and free of suffering. He quietly mouthed his last words to me, "I love you."

I related Alan's last hours and his death in the opening chapter of this book.

Our Doctor's Medical and Ethical Concerns
by Dr. Dora

I had been Alan's osteopath for many years and definitely noticed his mental decline. I usually saw him by himself, not with Phyllis; it was just the two of us in the room. When he began to consider avoiding the late stages of Alzheimer's by VSED, he discussed it with me several times. It never occurred to me that his wife might be pressuring him; he was in the process of making his own decision, and he was consistent with his desire. His primary concern was his own possible physical distress, and we discussed the specifics of how an attending doctor would be able to assure his comfort.

When it turned out that hospice would not agree to assist Alan with his VSED, Phyllis asked me if I would be the attending physician. I had already thought about the idea at some length, so that by the time she asked, I was pleased to agree to it right away. But I had a number of considerations and had thought it all through very carefully before this.

My first concern was my own inexperience with this type of care. That was alleviated when Phyllis arranged for a former hospice doctor to consult with me on the phone during Alan's process. I was also worried about my own legal liability, and that concern was handled when Phyllis's elder care attorney prepared a document that protected Phyllis, the caregivers, and me.

My other considerations were more complex. I am Catholic and don't believe in murder. Also, in some ways, Alan was "healthy." I would be assisting a strong body to deteriorate quickly.

The overriding principle for me that related to these two concerns was patient autonomy, a concept I had studied in a medical ethics course. Alan had a right to choose an elective death in his own home, and he had a right to treatment by a medical professional. I felt it would have been unethical for me to decline to assist my patient, whom I knew and trusted. Long ago, I had decided that an elective death by natural means is not murder, for the patient or the assisting doctor. I realized that my goal was to help Alan and keep him physically comfortable in his last days of life.

Even though I was well prepared for Alan's final journey, it still came as a shock for me, and it took me a long time to recover. In retrospect, I realize that part of what was difficult about Alan's departure was that, apart from his neurological disorder, I thought of him as healthy. A doctor would never say, "She is completely healthy except for her heart failure," or "He is completely healthy except for his kidney disease." Yet they do say, "He is completely healthy except for his Alzheimer's or MS." Doctors think of people with neurological disease as healthy if the rest of their body is healthy. That was Alan's state. He had a robust body. He had difficulty walking and had some rigidity, and he had lost affect. But he was what most doctors consider to be healthy. Yet, in a matter of nine and a half days, he went from this healthy state to being emaciated, stinking, shriveled, with end stage renal failure, and ultimately a coma. Even though I visited Alan often, the change was shocking, and it was with my support as a physician that he was able to endure this dramatic change.

Afterward, I had to re-evaluate whether what I had done was right. Once again, I kept returning to the patient autonomy principle and was comfortable that I had helped to make Alan's decisive choice for himself possible. Even when I concluded that I had done nothing wrong ethically, it still took me a number of months, perhaps even half a year, to get over witnessing the dramatic wasting of this otherwise healthy body.

Oregon was the first state in the Union to legalize

physician-assisted elective death. One year after it became legal there, it became one of the top ten causes of death in the state of Oregon. Because the Oregon Department of Health was required to investigate any new cause of death in the state, they undertook a thorough investigation of each and every case of physician assisted elective death in the previous year. Of course they were unable to interview any of the patients, but in each case, they interviewed family members, physicians, and hospital staff. Their conclusion was that none of the patients had been coerced, none had chosen elective death for the sake of their families, and none chose it for financial problems or for lack of success in healthcare. They had all long outlived life expectancy for their particular diagnosis.

Knowing this information helped me to cement my ideas about end-of-life issues. I feel that Oregon's Death with Dignity Act is too restricted. Patient autonomy should be the paramount consideration, and the Act should not restrict itself to specific terminal or degenerative diseases. Neurological diseases should not be excluded from the Death with Dignity option.

I have seen families devastated when a loved one is suffering from Alzheimer's. The person becomes unreliable, wanders off, gives away valuable possessions, may not even recognize family members, can behave like a frightened animal, and needs to be institutionalized. People who choose to end life voluntarily before having to endure this suffering or put their families through it should be permitted to do so.

I have always loved people passionately. I believe that is why I went into medicine. I care for people, and I enjoy helping others. I've always loved my patients tremendously. Alan was a handsome, otherwise healthy man. He was fun to be around. He was a good husband to Phyllis, and they had a wonderful marriage. It was hard to say goodbye to Alan, but I was willing to do that. I knew the time was drawing near when Alan would not be competent to make a decision. However, I felt he was very clear at the time when he started the VSED process and in the weeks leading up to his death. He was certain about his desire to end his life before he became mentally incompetent.

Other VSED Stories

Of course, every person's VSED experience will be different, as I learned by interviewing several other people who had helped loved ones with a VSED fast.

JoAnne

JoAnne contacted me in 2016 after her husband received his dementia diagnosis and they were in the process of clarifying his end of life wishes. He decided he wanted to VSED before he lost his mental competency. She said that my support, as they prepared for the initial appointment with their primary care physician, was invaluable. That appointment went well. Knowing they had the support of their doctor, they were able to move ahead with their lives.

JoAnne's husband's symptoms continued to progress over the following months. This had to do with issues of memory and spatial awareness. In late October 2016, they noticed a rapid increase in memory loss along with the loss of ability to read and remain focused in conversation. What was most frightening was the rapid onset of hallucinations and delusional episodes in which her husband was no longer able to recognize her or have any sense of reality. This made them realize that they had to move quickly if he was going to successfully achieve his end of life wish.

Having completed the preparations that I recommended, it was possible for them to move forward with their plan in spite of this man's progressive loss of cognition. Luckily, he was able to have the necessary conversation with his doctor so she could prescribe appropriate medications.

JoAnne's husband began his ten-day journey on December 5, 2016. He became agitated and confused in the first few days, and needed anti-anxiety and anti-psychotic medications in addition to the regular doses of morphine. With the proper medical support, he was able to achieve some calm and relaxation. He wanted to move around and even wanted to leave the house, which they couldn't allow him to do in his progressively weakened state. His ability to speak coherently was mostly gone by day three.

Although all food items were removed from sight, he went to the cupboard where they always had his favorite crackers. When he took down the box, his wife reminded him of what his wishes were, and he quickly returned the box to the shelf. Other than that, he never asked for food or anything more than a little moisture sprayed into his mouth. It was as if his commitment and determination were so deeply ingrained in his being that nothing could deter him.

Hospice took over his care after day four. Their added support, along with the twenty-four-hour caregiving support, made his final days peaceful and gentle. Their three children were present for his final days until his death.

Mary

Mary's mother was 92 when she decided to VSED because only at that age did she receive a diagnosis of Alzheimer's. She learned that the disease can progress rapidly later in life and became steadfast in her decision to VSED. They never signed any legal papers.

After she began her fast, she had no real pain or discomfort for a full week and then began using pain meds more because of restlessness than any true discomfort. She was up and brushing her teeth, sitting outside looking at the trees until the last couple of days. For the VSED process, Mary brought her mother home from the retirement center where she was living, because the center would not be involved in any way to support her fast. On the second day of the fast, a local hospice agreed to accept her mother, and hospice personnel came to Mary's apartment to help. Support by a private doctor or a hospice is ideal.

Mary had to endure judgments from some family members. She called me daily for support. I emphasized that surrounding herself with loving, fully supportive people was essential, because the process is exhausting, physically and emotionally. Mary's mother died on the eleventh day of her fast.

Lynn

In the case of Lynn, she had been diagnosed with Alzheimer's, and did a great deal of the preparation for VSED herself. She learned about VSED from hearing a presentation that I gave. She decided to VSED ten months before she began her fast and was still mentally competent during that time. She prepared for her fast by learning as much as she could about VSED. She read my website over and over (www.phyllisshacter.com), and was especially interested in what occurred in the nine and a half days that it took Alan to die.

She was a born organizer and worked hard to set everything up for her husband for when she was no longer there. She bought clothes for him, rearranged the house, stocked up on food, and asked him if he'd like her to dispose of her own clothes before she died. (He said that was not necessary.) She contacted everyone who was important to her one more time.

It was fairly easy for Lynn and her husband to set a date to begin the VSED process, because they had hired a death doula who kept a close eye on Lynn during the last months of her life. Lynn, her husband and the death doula were closely monitoring Lynn's mental deterioration and decided on the starting date together. The death doula orchestrated the VSED process, including the hiring of caregivers. Lynn's primary doctor stayed in close contact with the death doula and prescribed appropriate medication. Lynn's husband was able to continue sleeping in the same bed with her until she died because it was a large bed, and each side was adjustable. He was grateful that he had hired a death doula to orchestrate this process. He did whatever was requested of him.

One member of Lynn's immediate family did not support her decision to VSED and would not see her after she began her fast, but Lynn came to terms with this before she started to VSED.

One day toward the middle of her fast, Lynn woke up and said, "Am I dead yet?" She died the way she lived, a planner who liked to take control of situations, and who became impatient. She was well organized and had a good sense of humor. She died twelve days after she began her fast.

Joan

Joan's story was a bit different. She was accepted into a hospice facility, but it was one that had little experience with VSED. They could not provide consistent care because various staff members had different attitudes about VSED. Even though Joan's son requested that his Mom not be given liquids, if she asked for them, the staff did not follow her son's instructions. They even gave her orange juice. Part of the hospice philosophy is to give patients whatever they desire at the end of life. Finally, at the suggestion of the medical director, Joan was moved to her son's home to complete the VSED process, and she died there three days later.

Diane

Diane was in her late 80s and had already been on hospice care with late-stage cancer for several months. She had said goodbye to everyone, had reviewed her life, and felt ready to go. But she didn't die.

A friend of hers saw the film, *Speaking of Dying*, produced by Trudy James, in which I am interviewed about Alan's experience with VSED. The friend took the film to Diane, and they watched it together with Diane's daughter, who is a physician. Diane told her daughter she wanted to VSED and asked for her support. She stopped eating and drinking the next day and died peacefully in three days.

Ethel

Ethel was a piano player. After she had a series of strokes and had spent some time in a rehabilitation facility, she realized she would not be able to play the piano ever again and decided it was time for her to die. Her plan was to go home and stop eating and drinking, but she had no guidance about how to do this, and no medical support.

When she returned home, she had many visitors and flowers. Friends commented that she looked great. But she was still determined and proceeded with her fast.

After three days she became very thirsty and decided to stop the VSED process. She thought her daughter had told her that it would take her only three days to die, though the daughter denies ever saying this.

Discouraged about her inability to play the piano, three or four months later she started the VSED process again. This time, she did have professional help, and between a caregiver, a consulting physician, and her daughter, who this time was properly informed, she received proper medication and died peacefully.

A Final Word

The above cases are a reminder that thoughtful decision-making, excellent communications, professional caregiving, family support, and medical supervision are essential ingredients for a high quality VSED death.

The Caregiver's Daily Account with Medical Details

My friend Leslie Powell Shankman is a Certified Nursing Assistant who agreed to be the primary caregiver for Alan's fast. She alternated twelve-hour shifts with another CNA, Maymie Dixon, who had been one of Alan's caregivers for the previous five months. Leslie and Maymie kept a detailed log of the entire nine and a half days of Alan's VSED process. Below is Leslie's account of the background of her friendship with Alan and me, and then a day-by-day review of Alan's VSED process from a caregiver's point of view.

Summary of Daily Log
by Leslie Powell Shankman

I first met Phyllis and Alan in 2004 when we all attended an evening of participation in the Universal Dances for Peace program. I remember that these patterned circle dances lasted for about an hour and the whole time I danced next to Alan. That meant that half the time when we walked in one direction, I was following Alan. I didn't think much of it then since we all have different strengths, but I noticed that Alan seemed to have a hard time remembering and following the steps. Every move was a bit behind, a bit off, and done with some hesitation.

Not knowing him yet, I did actually wonder about his capacity after the dances were over. The whole time we had circled around a central display that consisted of a big round mirror on the floor with about 20 votive candles arranged on it, their flames dancing too. When the circle broke up Alan proceeded to walk across the floor and right through this central alter. Candles and wax scattered out in all directions as his unknowing feet kicked them asunder.

As I became friends with them over time, I learned that Alan was actually an incredibly intelligent and aware man and apparently had been quite the accomplished dancer. Poignantly, when Alzheimer's was diagnosed and I watched its hastening progression, I remembered this first meeting, seven years earlier, and realized that the shadowy specter of Alzheimer's had been stalking Alan even back then.

As Phyllis's friend, our usual get-togethers were long walks and talks in the neighboring woods—when we could find time. We were both busy people. I was working as a private caregiver and had a number of clients. Some of Phyllis's time was filled with fun community pursuits for her and Alan, but over the years that fun had progressively narrowed as Alan became more and more tired and health concerns took center stage. Phyllis was an incredibly supportive spouse, always right there for Alan, always investigating, always advocating.

After Alan chose his date to start VSED, I drew in closer to Phyllis. All my clients had died in succession the year prior and I was taking a break, thinking about moving on from caregiving. Being somewhat free, I told her I would work with her caregivers and help them think things through as well as collect all the supplies they'd need to have on hand as they anticipated the process. The start date was about two weeks hence. With this I suddenly entered not only the caregiver orbit, but the community orbit. The nearing of the date and the bold and forthright manner in which Phyllis had shared their plans, found many people suddenly spinning out. People spoke with each other, some spoke with me, and many flocked for guidance to the leader of the spiritual center that Alan was affiliated with. I spoke with her, too, about my stance with the various community members who had come to me, and even about my feelings. I was supportive of this decision, but still held a tinge of questioning. In short, there was electricity in the air, charged and raw. This was not an easy time for Phyllis. People questioned her, people doubted her, some thought she was forcing this on Alan. Her level of anxiety was off the charts—raw.

When I became involved with the caregivers, I quickly realized that the process could not be supported by the team that was in place. One caregiver was fine; she was perfect. I had worked closely with her before and had even sent her to Phyllis five months earlier when our mutual client died. She was everything a caregiver should be: loving, extremely technically competent, and, above all, knew how to listen. Her actions always came with deep regard for the dignity of the person she cared for. She loved Alan a lot, and she had used her time with him to closely observe him and do what he wanted and needed. She found that he consistently and genuinely spoke to her with a deep peace about his decision to VSED. And she knew that it was his decision.

The second caregiver was taking the lead in a very abrasive style and her understanding of the situation was too narrow. She felt that it was the job of the caregiving team to use their skills to get Alan through this. Since Phyllis was in such a state of high anxiety, this caregiver was issuing orders that Phyllis needed to back off and let the caregivers do their job. Phyllis should take a back seat and stay out of the way—go on walks, read books—keep busy or rest until the caregivers called on her. While this was perhaps a textbook solution to establishing what she felt would be good care, it was not a real life solution. In real life, this process demanded that a cocoon of love and reverence, as well as good care, surround Phyllis and Alan. Phyllis's instincts, coming from the deep bond that she and Alan shared, needed to be respected even when her anxiety seemed to push the bounds of "sensibility."

Once Phyllis saw the truth of these dynamics, she immediately released the second caregiver, who was telling Phyllis how to act. There was no equivocating for Phyllis. In her advocacy role and drawing on her fierce love for Alan, which so many misinterpreted, she knew that these dynamics would not support Alan, or her. This all added to the raw and chaotic tenor of the time. This walk was not for the faint of heart.

So, I stepped in as a caregiver and coordinator of the "team." I say "team" because I stepped in with the reflexive response that we would need some more help for this process. In my experience, I had found it to be optimum to have a coordinated team of three, four, or even five interchangeable people in place for a twenty-four hour care situation. Each caregiver would have a set schedule, but within that we could trade and flex with each other without creating a gap for the client. I knew two caregivers who also knew Phyllis and Alan and who were aligned with supporting them, so I immediately engaged them and set up a schedule for the first four or five days.

Within the first forty-eight hours I realized that this was not a usual situation and this full team approach was not necessary or beneficial. The VSED care process asks for a different kind of response. The reality is that although it will be a demanding few weeks for all, a successful and well-managed VSED process will be over in two to three weeks. The dying person's needs will change rapidly within this short span of time. Caregivers need to be in sync with the client, with the doctor, and with the surrounding family and friends. More is not better in this case. Two or three hearty souls who can tunnel in for the duration and who can know themselves as a team are better. The communication between caregivers, as one shift ends and another begins, helps them to stay current with the variables of the dying process. Since the foundational bedrock of the process is maintaining an emotionally supportive environment, the smooth functioning of the care team is essential. Thus, it quickly became evident that in this case, my working twelve hours and trading off with my former colleague would work best. So, I released the two newly acquired team members.

When Alan started his process on April 10, 2013, Phyllis had decided that care would not be necessary that first day during the daylight hours. She was correct. Alan basically went to his room and stayed there. I started at 8:00 that evening to cover the night shift. Before I turn to the specifics of the days and their progression, I want to say that these first few days took us all by surprise. In these first days, Alan—who had barely been able to stay awake for more than eight hours a day for the last several years now, and only with the help of some stimulant doses of Ritalin—was now fully awake, engaged, and even perky. This created total cognitive dissonance. Speaking for myself, this was really hard. I could not imagine that this enlivened man was actually going to be dead within a few weeks. It was hard to grasp that he could get from here to there.

Thankfully the doctor supplied rationality when she explained this reaction as the temporary effect of ketosis. My human mind needed to cope with all this by being very present in the moment and being open to going with what each moment would bring while holding strong to the over-riding pursuit. I must reflect on Phyllis here again. This was a Herculean task for her. While the moments and changes were met by extreme anxiety and constant questioning from her, she had an unwavering core of purpose that she never lost sight of in supporting Alan to his end. Any care team supporting VSED serves themselves and the client best by making it their purpose to act with patience and compassion, not only for the client, but for the entire matrix of family surrounding the client. That is why the caregiver who just wanted Phyllis to "get out of the way" so she could do her job by supporting Alan was so inappropriate.

Now let us descend into the progression of days, and nights, to understand the moment-to-moment details of Alan's journey.

Day One

As I mentioned, Phyllis correctly decided a caregiver was not needed this first day. Alan stayed in his room busying himself with a few familiar pursuits. In fact, for the first two to three days he followed the habits of living by keeping himself busy watching Seinfeld shows on his small DVD player (the same few over and over), listening to music or to NPR, "reading" the *New Yorker*, or sleeping. It felt to me like these familiar rituals were his way of grounding. Of course, Phyllis spent time with him, too. But generally, in this first phase, it seemed to be more comforting to Alan to engage in these pursuits by himself.

The doctor came and spoke with Alan and he told her that he wanted to start the process with as little medication as possible. She examined him.

Night One

I covered the first night. I stayed outside of his room but set up a baby monitor to listen for activity. I also set my phone alarm to be sure I woke up intermittently in case I fell into too deep a sleep. It was an uneventful night. I did respond to noise about 2:30 AM and found that Alan had just finished using the handheld urinal—he also had a bedside commode. The bathroom was only steps away, but we knew that with the progression of his process we would need all these options before eventually going to adult diapers when he could no longer get up.

Alan was alert and conversant but at one point I found him sort of half-off and half-on the bed. Had he been trying to get fully up and unable to? I took the urinal from him and helped him back into bed. I did have to wonder what he would have done with the urinal had I not come in to take it at that point.

The doctor's initial orders were to offer Alan a small dose of morphine (.1 ml) every two hours to keep him comfortable. Phyllis administered this during the first day. At night the orders were to give the morphine upon awaking but not to purposely awaken him for the two-hour cycle. So I swabbed Alan's mouth for comfort and gave him the morphine while he was up. I could see that he was feeling the mouth and jaw pain that was a constant for him from previous dental work and that, in recent weeks, had been treated with Vicodin. With the start of VSED, the Vicodin was discontinued so this initial small amount of morphine actually served as a replacement response for his pain.

Alan settled down after all this and went back to sleep until 8:20 AM. Phyllis went in to be with him then. They had always had a rhythm of coming together in what they considered special sharing time upon awakening, and the VSED process did not alter that, but made it all the more precious.

Several care functions were constant during each shift and were done repeatedly. One priority was to keep the cool mist humidifier filled with water so it would run continuously. This added valuable moisture to the air and helped in a small way to offset the effects that dehydration has on skin, lips, and eyes. We also kept Alan's lips moistened with a good quality lip moisturizer and his eyes moistened with no-preservative artificial tears. Lotion was routinely applied to his skin, especially his face.

For the first few days we used soaked sponge sticks to moisten and clean his mouth and this was done routinely for comfort. Over the days though, as Alan became thirstier, we found that Alan aggressively sucked on the sponges. This was alarming for two reasons. First, upon squeezing the moisture out of the sponges we realized they held quite a lot of water. The teaspoons to tablespoon he was getting so many times a day was actually adding up significantly. In addition, it is dangerous when a patient clamps down on these sponges on a stick. With enough force the sponge can be bitten off the stick and become a choking hazard. The sponges are still valuable for oral care but should be used along the outer tooth surfaces. If the client can keep his mouth open or extrude his tongue, they can be used to clean the tongue and inner tooth surfaces. Realizing all this, we later switched to using a small one-ounce spray bottle to spray mists of water into Alan's mouth.

Sometimes we put *Bach's Rescue Remedy* into the water glass that we soaked the sponge in. This is a mixture of flower essences that can be used to help in stressful situations. *Rescue Remedy* helps one to relax, focus, and feel calm. Flower essences contain the energetic, or vibrational nature, of the flower, which is transmitted to the user. Because it is a vibrational remedy, there is no concern about mixing the essences with the medications that are used. *Rescue Remedy* can also be added to the water in the spray bottle.

Day Two

This day was covered by one of the new caregivers I had hired. All went smoothly with Alan either staying in his room engaging in his familiar pursuits or napping.

However, there was some lack of clarity about giving the small amount of morphine at the two-hour intervals versus asking Alan if he wanted it, so she asked each time. His answer was "no" so she heeded that.

While the baby monitor was set up to listen in, we realized Alan actually needed to be watched as he would occasionally move in and out of the hospital bed. His movements were awkward and we did not want a fall to cause an injury that might waylay his process. So, we placed a recliner in the hallway near his open door. This allowed the caregiver to watch him. The presence was not intrusive, and Alan did not seem to be aware of or be bothered by this.

Per doctor's order, one suppository was administered during this shift. If there were no results in thirty minutes, we were to administer another. It worked so we didn't need to.

Night Two

This evening was covered by the second new caregiver I had engaged. As the team coordinator, I had been checking in on how it was going. We had established that it was not advisable to ask Alan if he wanted morphine. We found that without the low steady dose his various pains emerged and we got into the position of "chasing pain" rather than being on top of it. So during the night shift, the caregiver entered his room and gave the morphine dose every two hours.

I don't remember if this was a team decision, but in looking back at the notes, doctor's orders were not to awaken Alan during the night to give the morphine, but to administer upon natural awakening. Thus keeping to the schedule was the caregiver's interpretation of what to do. It was a logical choice in light of our earlier decision to stay with a schedule to avoid chasing pain. The care log shows that Alan awoke each time she administered the morphine at which time he got up, with her assistance, to urinate or defecate before returning back to sleep.

Having two caregivers take opposite approaches over twenty-four hours underscores why I decided that having more caregivers was not warranted. With communication over time, a team comes into sync with each other and all these details smooth out. With the short nature of VSED and with the rapidly changing, sometimes charged, course of care, I could see that it would be easier and more coherent to work with one other caregiver. As coordinator, I needed to check in regularly anyway, even when not on shift myself. It only made sense to dive in and commit fully to the hours and the process.

Day Three

I was on again. I spoke to both of the new caregivers and we all accepted that it would be more realistic for them to disengage. Going forward I would handle the day shifts and my partner would take the evening shifts.

I started the shift thinking that we needed to plan on going for a more thorough bodily clean up. Alan was still fairly steady on his feet and it might be the last day he could take a shower. He was too sleepy in the morning so I didn't push it. When he eventually wanted to get up around noon I stood by to guide him to the toilet and had him use his cane for stability. It became clear that he had no interest, and perhaps not adequate energy, for a shower. I gave him a washcloth so he could wash his own face at the sink. Then he did his own oral care. Afterward, he sat on the closed toilet and I used the cloth and the sink water to wash his back. I gave him the cloth to wash under his arms and chest. Then I took it to reach his legs and feet. He applied deodorant and I helped him put on a new undershirt, boxers, and socks.

His bed was straightened and refreshed with a new

continence pad. Although we applied lip moisturizer regularly, Alan's lips were now starting to get dry. His face was also becoming dry, and we applied a special cream prepared by Phyllis from coconut oil and shea butter. After this flurry of activity, Alan seemed happy to return to bed. It was clear that hygiene would be done with washcloths from now on, either integrated into times he toileted or as a bed bath.

This was the day that Adult Protective Services showed up unannounced, responding to claims of elder abuse. Alan looked very fresh and well cared for when the social worker met with him.

Around 4:00 PM, Alan wanted to get up again in response to the urge to urinate. He was less steady on his feet. He tried to urinate but there was no result. He was starting to have the stinging feeling in the urethra that one gets with a bladder infection and he was uncomfortable. I called the doctor to report. Her first impulse was to order a medication used to eliminate the stinging feeling. She called back shortly to say that the med was not available in a liquid form. Tablets were out of the question since Alan could not use water to swallow them. To address the discomfort, the doctor adjusted the morphine to .2ml every two hours in the daytime and .2ml during the night if he awoke. Within a few hours the increased dose of morphine removed his discomfort and Alan was able to urinate without pain.

The reality of caregiving is that caregivers need to overlap shifts somewhat. There are some things, such as changing the bed with the patient in it, that are easier done with two people. Time is also needed to brief each other and confer on plans for best care. Thus, my partner arrived a bit early at the end of my day so that we could work together to comfortably administer two suppositories for Alan. Since he had tolerated the one yesterday without cramping, the doctor wanted us to use two. Again, Alan had results.

Night Three
This was an uneventful evening with Alan sleeping well from 10:00 PM until 5:45 AM. The slight increase in morphine seemed effective. He was not in pain, had no stinging in his urethra, and upon waking did not need toileting despite having gone the whole night without getting up. After some mouth swabbing and lip ointment, Alan went back to sleep for a few more hours. The log reports that he seemed at peace this morning.

Day Four
Alan awoke again on my shift at 8:45 AM. I gave him the .2ml of morphine, the first dose since 8:00 PM last evening. I assisted Alan to the toilet and stood back by the door to give him some privacy since he told me he had both urges. We had a little bell for Alan to use when he wanted help, so I gave that to him asking him to ring it when he was finished. An ever-present question in caregiving is how to best strike the balance between support and care on the one hand, without completely taking over and denying the patient his or her dignity and autonomy on the other. Our ideals were too lofty here, for Alan could not really remember and track the idea of ringing a bell. And as the hours went by and he was becoming weaker we would soon have to act on the side of safety and forgo the idea of autonomy. I did not hear the bell but heard the water running. I stepped in to find Alan standing at the sink with the faucet on. He dipped his head down and took a big mouthful of water. Before he swallowed I told him he should really spit it out but that it was his choice. He swallowed it and flashed me a devilish grin. Back in bed he went right to sleep. The effects of dehydration were starting to become more evident.

Alan awoke a few hours later asking that his mouth be

swabbed. I asked him about jaw, urethra, and back pain. He answered that those pains were not bothering him but the mouth dryness was. Although he answered no to pain, his body and gestures suggested a different answer. Verbal communication is not the most reliable measure for a person with compromised memory who is becoming dehydrated. I could see that we had reached the point where we needed to start responding to nonverbal signs of discomfort. These signs include, but are not limited to, grimacing, moaning, restlessness, moving hands towards the face, moving the mouth or jaw with or without noise, and restless leg movements. Alan was starting to exhibit all of these in some measure. I rubbed his back for a while and, fortuitously, the doctor made a house call.

Seeing all his motions signaling discomfort, the doctor increased his morphine to .4ml every two hours and gave orders that it be given at night when he woke up. If the .4ml did not calm him, we had orders to increase the dose to .6 ml every two hours. She also put in an order for a 25mcg fentanyl patch and explained that when that came in and was applied later in the day it would gradually release medication and build up to a level equal to the morphine dose. The morphine would then be adjusted down or eliminated, per need.

Later, in reviewing the arc of care, I could see how well the doctor anticipated and managed Alan's needs throughout the full course of his dying process. He was fully conscious as he wanted to be in the beginning. As dehydration and discomfort set in, those symptoms were addressed in accordance with his original wishes—an artful plan that kept him comfortable but not overmedicated.

By early evening Alan was a lot more settled and appeared comfortable. This lasted until he had the urge to urinate. I helped him to the bedside commode but despite sitting for ten minutes there was no urine to pass. Back in bed, he was finally able to urinate a while later, this time staying in bed and using the urinal. His urine was by now very dark and starting to be orange in color.

This evening we again followed the doctor's orders and administered two suppositories. He mainly passed gas and liquid. Before the end of my shift, the fentanyl patch arrived and we needed to clip his stomach hair short, wash and dry the area well, and apply the patch to the left of his belly button.

At the end of the shift I noted in the log that Alan had been awake most of the day. For most of the day he had a "thinking" look with his hands often resting on his face or head. He was very calm except for the restless peak before the morphine dosage was increased.

Night Four

Alan slept from 9:00 PM until shortly after midnight when he awoke exhibiting restlessness. Oral moisture and morphine were given and Alan fell back asleep until 3:30 AM. This time he had the urge to urinate. At first there were no results, but finally, sitting up on the side of the bed with the urinal in hand he was able to go. The caregiver had to support his back so he could sit up in this manner. She gave him another dose of morphine and he went back to sleep.

Although we maintained the baby monitor in his room and had our phone alarms on, as I noted earlier, the caregiver sat stationed in the recliner with Alan fully in view. This was important because as Alan became progressively weaker he had no discernment about his weakness. So, in response to an urge and perhaps also by the force of habit, Alan would try to get out of bed by himself. At 7:55 AM, when he awoke again, the caregiver found him trying to get out of bed. Again he wanted to urinate. She helped him stand to use the urinal and he had results.

As we always did proactively when he was awake, she swabbed his mouth and applied lip balm. She did not give a dose of morphine because by now the fentanyl patch had taken over giving the equivalent of a steady dose of .4-.5 ml of morphine, almost the .6 ml he had worked up to before the patch. The doctor had given us specific orders on how to supplement with morphine for signs of pain or distress. With these cares done, Alan went back to sleep.

Day Five

When Alan awoke again he was very thirsty. I called on Phyllis to address this with him. She did this by reminding him what he was trying to do and gave him a choice of water or spray mists. He chose the mist. But Phyllis, so alert and proactive about Alan's comfort, asked him if he wanted to receive a little more medication so he could be comfortable beyond his thirst. Alan now wanted this. Phyllis called the doctor and a new plan was put into place.

This was a day of adjusting doses of the fentanyl and morphine to look for that "sweet spot" of balance and comfort. Lorazepam was added to the mix. The doctor wanted us to have this medication on board for its calming effect when needed, but also because of its effective response to seizures. Dehydration in the elderly can make them more prone to seizures and should that happen to Alan, she wanted the antidote close by.

Alan went into a deeper sleep for a while. At 10:30 AM he awoke and Phyllis asked him if he was still thirsty. He shook his head "no."

I went into the kitchen to join Phyllis and a friend. Soon after, Alan wobbled out with a cane and a "boyish" smile on his face. He said he had to pee. I assisted him into the bathroom. His urine was dark and orange. I helped him back into bed.

While we worked on the medication levels, we also

realized that we now needed to employ a two-pronged approach with Alan. The time to be verbal with him was past. Questions were just confusing. Besides using medication, we needed to support him with presence and touch. He no longer wanted the solitude to follow his "busy" pursuits as he had in the first few days. Now he seemed to want company. Phyllis's friend knew a pressure point type of massage, and with her guidance, she and I held different calming points on his body. It was determined that someone would sit quietly with him most of the time now, resting a hand somewhere on his body. It seemed to ground and reassure him, and his looks of appreciation toward whoever was sitting with him affirmed that he welcomed this.

Medication adjustments were guided by his reactions. In the afternoon, he felt the urge to urinate but couldn't. His face and neck became red and itchy. His eyes seemed drier. The urge to pee had him trying to get out of bed to get to the toilet. He was very weak, so I put on a gait belt and he leaned on his walker. With a visiting friend spotting him on his other side, I assisted him to the bedside commode. He was finally able to pee and the urine was now very orange.

These times of getting up would soon end, but while he still could do it, even with heavy assistance, we allowed him some movement, circulatory stimulation, and relief from pressure points. This also provided an opportunity to clean him and the bed. I changed the bed linens and refreshed the draw sheets/continence pads. I also took this opportunity to clean Alan's body more adequately. Using washcloths, I completed a thorough peri-wash as he stood with his walker. Later, as he sat on the closed commode, I washed and lotioned his face and body. We applied deodorant and put a clean shirt on him.

Once Alan was back in bed I positioned him comfortably.

When we moved Alan now we noticed that his legs were getting stiffer. The doctor thought that Alan probably also had Parkinson's. This seemed likely as he had the shuffling walk, the flat facial affect, and the leg stiffness that I had so often seen in others with the disease.

It was now necessary to prop his feet. This is called "floating the heels" since the heels don't touch the mattress when it is done correctly. Pressure sores can happen so quickly, and the heels are especially prone to breaking down if they rest too long on the mattress. I kept his socks off so his feet could be easily monitored for pressure spots.

In the evening, Alan had a slight fever. The fever is another sign of the increasing dehydration.

Alan sees Phyllis and says weakly, "Can I help you?"

Night Five

Doctor's orders are to administer some of the meds during the night even if Alan is asleep. This is motivated by the new goal to keep him comfortable beyond his thirst. Since Alan is now being assisted with positioning in bed, a turn schedule is followed so that he is not lying on any one area long enough to develop skin breakdown and pressure sores. During the night, we just turned him side to side as it is easier to administer the morphine into the back of his cheek pocket while he is sleeping. With his automatic hospital bed we can adjust the head level as needed. Administering the morphine while he is on his side also reduces the risk of aspiration, which can happen more easily when given while on his back.

Depending on the dose and the amount of the liquid in the syringe, sometimes the medicine needs to be administered in intervals. To do this we insert the syringe into the back lower cheek pocket and depress the plunger just a little to let a small amount come out. Then we remove the syringe from the mouth and hold it casually up as if holding a cigarette at bay before the next inhale. This is repeated several times until the syringe is empty. In this way the medicine can trickle down the throat even if the patient's swallowing isn't fully engaged. It is really unnerving to have too much medicine seem to go down the wrong way and cause a fit of choking. And the choking brings on the potential to aspirate.

The fentanyl patches were a welcome addition as Alan progressed because they reduced the need to administer ever-larger doses of the liquid medicine.

Although Alan was receiving a greater amount of medication, the doctor was quite prudent. We had detailed orders to count Alan's breaths per minute before we gave doses and were to skip the dose if his breath count was below ten. Sometimes it was easier to get an accurate breath count by laying a hand on his chest, thereby following the rise and fall of his breath.

Day Six

By the morning Alan was fairly sedated. When he tried to speak, it was gibberish. The doctor later explained that this speech was a side effect of the Lorazepam. Before the night caregiver left, we tended to Alan together. He was now wearing disposable tab diapers and he needed a new one and thorough peri-care. Anti-fungal cream was applied to irritated areas and barrier cream to others.

The doctor made a house call soon after. She checked Alan, taking his vitals and looking at his skin for pressure spots. Alan's lungs were clear. She advised that we watch for scratching from his hands on his face and if it looked like he was scratching we should file his nails down and even cover them if necessary. Then the doctor did a full neurological exam. She determined that we had reached the desired sedation level and that the fentanyl patches were covering the release of medication at an appropriate level so that the morphine and Lorazepam could be discontinued.

In the early afternoon, a friend of Alan's came to visit. She helped me with his care. Together we did the peri-care and ointments, brief change, and turning. Alan opened his eyes and, seeing her, made little kissing gestures. After we cleaned him up Phyllis went in and spent a long time with Alan.

Just three hours after his last care, we changed his briefs and did peri-care. Although he was dehydrated, water was leaving Alan's body. Alan opened his eyes during this and made some responses.

Night Six

Again we performed the complete peri-care and washing. We changed the bedding as well. Alone or together, changing Alan was necessary at regular intervals throughout the day and night. Sometimes when we turned him, it would cause urine to leak and that would necessitate a change.

Alan's eyes were becoming quite dry. The cool mist humidifier was still going. We had been administering preservative-free artificial tears at intervals, but they now seemed to be irritating his eyes. The doctor advised us to put a cool washcloth over his eyes. She also advised that we start applying Genteal Liquid Eye Gel every two hours. We did this for just awhile as it became moot when Alan started keeping his eyes closed most of the time. The medications and breath counting were continued at intervals during the night shift. The turn schedule was followed every two hours and the mouth misting and lip care continued. Alan talked a little when awake. Overall, he seemed comfortable.

Day Seven

My care partner and I overlapped so we could tend to Alan. He was soaking wet this morning. We gave him a bed bath, lotioned his skin, applied the barrier creams, and administered two suppositories. Even when dying, a person continues to release waste and produce stool. Without drinking or eating, normal movement of the large intestine diminishes. Pain medication also slows the movement of the intestine, so a person can easily become constipated with hard stool. This causes abdominal pain. Suppositories help clear the colon of stool so the person can remain comfortable.

In the afternoon, Alan was able to open his eyes and purse his lips and give little kisses in the air.

Phyllis spent a lot of time in bed with Alan today. Alan was responsive with her and at one point pointed to his mouth to indicate that he needed some moisture. Once he received it, he whispered, "Better."

This is the day that Alan "rallied." This is often common a few days before death. A person will appear to be declining and nearing death, and then suddenly with a burst of mystifying energy become interactive and observant and seem more alive. Alan spoke with Phyllis in a lot of meaningful metaphorical language during his rally. He said, "The show is going to start... the people are at the party...time to go..." reflecting his impending transition. He also moved his arms around gesturing and reaching out into the netherworlds, as can be so typical prior to death. Hospice nurses refer to this as "Nearing Death Awareness."

Night Seven

This night was comfortable with the medication, breath counting, brief changing, and repositioning continuing at intervals. The evening caregiver is a gifted "energy worker" and during her shift, she often gently worked on Alan as he slept. She noted that Alan coughed occasionally and it sounded like fluid might be starting to accumulate in his lungs.

Day Eight

We started the day with our usual shift overlap so we could clean Alan and refresh the bed. Then Alan went back to sleep and Phyllis went in to spend the morning by his side. By noon Alan needed to be changed, cleaned, and repositioned. His body felt warm so I left the blanket off, covering him only with the sheet. Since the care process can be so jostling, especially as the patient becomes more inert, I asked Phyllis to come back in after I finished so we could stand, me with hands on his feet and she with hands on his head. This is a soothing and grounding gesture for most patients.

As Phyllis watched Alan, she asked him to blink if he was comfortable. Even though his eyelids were closed, he squeezed his eyes, and she was happy for this positive response.

Later, as Phyllis lay in bed with Alan, she told him that she loved him. He was able to mouth "I love you" back. These were his last words to her. It seemed as though he was starting to go into his end of life coma. I continued with the needed bodily care and medications throughout the day.

Night Eight

Care now consisted of turning Alan's body, keeping him clean, and administering the well-orchestrated medications at varying times in response to changing needs and signs. The night was busy but routine. Alan was less responsive so his needs were different. We were into the subtleties of care. Tonight Alan's lungs started to cackle, the first signs of fluid build-up, so it was important to keep the head of his bed raised a bit.

Day Nine

Alan slept comfortably into the morning hours and we could hear the rattling in his lungs. His sister called mid-morning. We put the phone to his ear so he could hear her. He raised his eyebrow in response.

By 1:00 PM, Alan was breathing shallowly but in a regular, even rhythm at thirteen breaths a minute. He started coughing intermittently, a very wet sounding cough. I put my hand on his chest and felt a wheeze and listened to the cackling sound of the fluid building in his lungs. Watching him, I saw that when he coughed, his face moved into a stressed, pained grimace. Within thirty minutes, he was wincing consistently, and the fluid sounds were more pronounced, accompanied by gasps and "yerp" sounds.

I had Phyllis come in to ask Alan if he wanted pain relief. He squeezed his eyes in the "yes" signal. In response, I gave him the supplemental morphine and called the doctor to report. She gave me new orders on what to watch for and how to medicate in response. Meanwhile, I could see already that this one dose of morphine had made Alan more comfortable.

We followed the protocol and by early evening Alan was resting very comfortably.

Night Nine

We overlapped shifts to care for Alan. He started the evening comfortably. He slept peacefully, breathing fourteen breaths a minute, with no gurgling sounds. The caregiver administered the meds every two hours as the doctor had ordered.

Shortly after midnight, the caregiver felt a distinct shift. Alan's breathing became more shallow and irregular and his heartbeat was fast, now at 120 beats per minute. Phyllis was awakened as she had left instructions to be alerted whenever there was a change. She crawled into bed next to Alan. The caregiver administered the next two doses of medication as scheduled, but Alan's neck felt perceptibly hard and it seemed like the medication was not going down, as if there was no response to swallow or let the liquid trickle in. She called the doctor at this point to report the changes. Phyllis, concerned about the lack of swallowing, asked if the next dose of medication could be withheld.

The caregiver spoke with the doctor again in the early morning and received new medication instructions. Alan's heartbeat was now at 138 beats per minute and his breath was faster at nineteen per minute.

Day Ten

I arrived early to debrief with my partner. She showed me how to best position Alan to administer the medication now that he seemed unable to swallow it. Alan's feet were cold and his back and head were sweaty. During the morning Alan's breath ranged from fourteen to seventeen breaths per minute and his pallor was a pale white with a blue tinge. By 11:00 AM his breath had slowed to ten breaths a minute with some long pauses. The doctor had instructed that we withhold the medication if his breath slowed to this pace, so I did.

It felt like Alan was no longer really in his body, even though his body lay right there in front of us breathing. A very good friend of Alan's came over, and I led her into the room to be with him. It was interesting because as we walked into the room, there was a distinct feeling, almost a sound, that we both felt so strongly that we looked at each other immediately with that inner question of, "Did you feel that!?" In response, she said to me, "He knows I'm here." The feeling/sound can be compared to the sound of the apparatus cycling water in a fish tank releasing a flush of water with a distinct "bloo-oop" as new water comes in. It was almost like the whole room was "full of Alan," and when we walked into it, our entry into "him" caused the "bloo-oop" sound.

At noon the doctor arrived to examine Alan. His heart rate was up to 150 beats a minute. She performed a complete neurological exam and declared that Alan's brain functions were basically gone except for the automatic response of his brain stem keeping his systems going. She adjusted the medication orders, stopping the morphine, scheduling some Lorazepam, and anticipating another fentanyl patch. She consulted with a fellow physician by phone for feedback and told us that, given the health and strength of Alan's heart, we might expect that he could live for forty-eight to seventy-two more hours.

As a caregiver I had been part of this phase of dying a number of times. Based on past experience, I was guessing forty-eight hours. Physiologically, the heart goes on until it wears itself out, with systems shutting down along the way, and finally the last breath comes. The patient is effectively gone at this point, in a deep coma, but the shutdown of body systems takes time. It is always hard because the end has come but has not quite arrived, and all who accompany their loved one are in a suspended, seemingly never-ending limbo state.

After the doctor left, a visiting neighbor and I went in to tend to Alan. I noticed his right foot was now mottled blue. I needed to clean him up, change his brief, and turn him again. She kindly helped, holding Alan to the side with the draw sheet so I could care for him in a smoother, less jostling manner. We even changed his shirt. Many days ago we had cut several T-shirts down the back so they could be easily slipped on and off as one would a hospital gown.

After we finished Phyllis came in. She wanted to be alone with Alan and shut the door. She felt very disturbed; it did not feel right to her that he was no longer really in his body, and yet his body persisted.

The neighbor and I went into the kitchen and talked a bit. After ten minutes or so, she remarked at how stuffy it felt in the house. She suggested that I open the back door and she open the front. The doors were a distance from each other but almost mirrored each other in position. As we simultaneously opened the doors a strong cross ventilation of air blew in and through the house. It was literally a strong fresh wind. Feeling it, my mind spontaneously said, "Go ahead Alan, you can go out on the wind." As this thought completed, Phyllis exited Alan's room in a state of awe and shock. She said, "He did it, he's gone, I helped mid-wife him home, he did it...."

We called the doctor and she came over. At 2:42 PM she wrote: "Patient is expired" along with other medical terminology. The up-to-seventy-two hours for the expected time of death had taken not more than a half-hour.

When things quieted down, Phyllis and I washed Alan's body in a thoughtful ritualistic way, thanking his body for all the ways it had served him. Phyllis added her special prayers and thoughts for Alan. He looked absolutely beautiful. It was as if a special glow came out of him and he was so, so handsome. He looked decades younger and Phyllis marveled at the echo of his younger physical self that now lay before us. The odyssey of their twenty-six years of love and dedication shone from this radiant dead body.

We made Alan ready for the arrival of the death mid-wife and for further special preparations. His body was kept at home for the next seventy-two hours in a ritual vigil, but he was not in the limbo between life and death. He was fully released and had moved on.

CHAPTER FIVE
Our Cancer Story

Our experience with Alan's decision to choose elective death rather than live into the late stages of Alzheimer's was complicated by his almost simultaneous cancer diagnosis. I am including our cancer story here because it is an unusual one with some aspects that I believe will be helpful to others. Cancer statistics often dismiss unexplainable, "spontaneous" healing, or healing by means of alternative, non-allopathic treatments, as irrelevant, so rare that they are not worth counting—or studying. Yet these are probably exactly the cases that researchers should pay attention to, the cases that could open up effective but lesser-known healing modalities. Alan's complete cure from cancer in four months was one the health establishment considered to be a "miracle." Doctors were astonished. However, we viewed it to be the result of our fierce commitment to and belief in the "alternative" treatments we chose.

In February 2012, about two months after Alan had been diagnosed with laryngeal cancer, at dinner one night, I asked him: "When are you going to be healed from cancer? He hesitated and then said, "March." I said, "March? No, that's so soon. I think it will be June . . . June 8. I can reserve the Center for Spiritual Living, and we can celebrate and publicly tell people how you healed." As it turned out, Alan was right! He began to feel stronger by mid-March and his voice returned. At our April visit to the oncologist, his cancer was gone! And then, we did celebrate his healing on June 8 with our community of friends. Here is how the story unfolded.

The Cancer Treatments

Alan's throat surgeon announced that Alan required three invasive throat surgeries. Here is his verbatim e-mail to us:

> If you don't choose this treatment, the cancer will definitely rob you of your ability to swallow, to breathe, and to speak. Although the surgery risks your laryngeal functions, the cancer will, with certainty, take all three functions away and cause a great deal of discomfort. I can't predict the timeline for your cancer if it is untreated. You could develop significant symptoms as soon as two or three months or at best in six to twelve months. Delaying treatment will increase the extent of surgery needed, and decrease the chance of a cure. Even with the surgery, there is a thirty percent chance that you will not be able to breathe, speak, or swallow.

The doctor made no mention of the Alzheimer's.

We scheduled the first surgery and went to the pre-operative appointment at the hospital. But while we were waiting three weeks for the surgery to occur, we talked and talked. We realized that surgery was the only tool in our surgeon's toolbox, but that many other treatment possibilities did in fact exist. Both of us had studied and used complementary healing modalities successfully for many years. We were also well aware of what traditional doctors called "spontaneous healings," complete recoveries that occur relatively quickly and cannot be explained by the medical profession. We both believed that disease is not only about the body, but also about the mind and our ways of relating to life.

Alan made a bold decision: "There will be no surgery!"

We left the medical maze of allopathic medicine and focused intensely on naturopathy, prayer, and visualization. I had learned how to oversee a health team when I became an advocate for my mother in her last years of life and was comfortable working with a team of professionals. They all knew about each other, and I coordinated their treatments. Because Alzheimer's had taken away Alan's sharp memory, I had to supervise everything. I became like a drill sergeant making sure Alan followed the entire protocol. My day started before Alan's and ended after he went to bed. Not only was I physically exhausted, I was heartbroken because I could see I was losing my beloved husband. Alan was sick with both cancer and Alzheimer's and became more withdrawn than ever before.

The naturopath prescribed a diet based on Alan's particular needs, but since it was a healthy diet, I decided to follow it as well so Alan would not be lured by other food in the house. The diet was not a challenge for us because, throughout our marriage, we had tried almost every diet that came along. At various times, we had tried food combining and eating only fruit until noon. We were vegetarian and then vegan. We tried eating a no fat diet, and later, we tried eating meat and lots of fat. For a while, we tried eating only raw food and raw dairy, then we ate the foods that were prescribed for our blood type. We tried it all—and none of it prevented Alan from contracting both cancer and Alzheimer's!

In addition to the diet, our naturopath prescribed many

supplements. Each day I prepared them in the morning then administered them to Alan on a schedule all day long, from the moment he arose until just before he went to bed. He also had to do enemas throughout the week. It was intense.

Our naturopathic clinic does not treat cancer; it treats the underlying causes of disease, including viruses, bacteria, parasites, mold, fungus, and heavy metals. They also like their patients to see a biological dentist who focuses on the implications of oral health on the wellbeing of the entire body. Our biological dentist said Alan needed to have nine teeth removed, including seven root canals. Alan complied.

We employed two more healing techniques that were part of the mix that cured Alan's cancer: group prayer and visualization. Alan wrote an affirmative prayer, which I sent to many friends and family members with a request that they say the prayer with us every evening at 7:30 Pacific Time. The prayer was written in the present tense with the understanding that the healing was occurring every evening in real time. At least seventy-five people poured out this prayer with us, all at the same time, for four months. Every night following the prayer, I practiced Therapeutic Touch on Alan's throat area, a healing modality that Alan and I learned from nurses in the 1990s.

This is the letter and prayer we sent to the prayer circle.

Here is Alan's request for your prayerful intentions. How you pray is perfect. Whatever God means to you is perfect. Use whatever you want for the word "God." We will all be doing the nightly prayer at 7:30 pm. If you are not able to do this at 7:30 pm, then please do it as close to that time as possible. We will be doing this together for four months. Please start this on Sunday, January 8th. Studies have proven that this type of simultaneous group prayer is very effective.

"I put my faith and trust in the flow of God's grace for Alan Alberts. I know that the Spirit of God flows in, though, and around Alan, in every cell and every dimension. Every part of Alan's body knows what to do and how to do it perfectly with ease so that he is free of cancer now. Alan feels well and has vitality. Alan has enough energy to play music on Sundays at Woodside Spiritual Center. I hold Alan in the Love and Light of God for whatever are Alan's highest and best good."

Throughout the four months, Alan visualized his healing and his next visit to the doctor's office in great detail. He visualized how he felt, what he heard, and what he saw as the surgeon threaded the fiber-optic cable through his nose until the end of it reached his vocal cords, the location where the cancer had been. In his visualization, he heard the doctor say, "The cancer is gone!" Then he imagined a feeling of enormous gratitude wash through him. Just as Wayne Dyer said in the book, *Wishes Fulfilled*, Alan imagined his future dream as a present reality by experiencing the feeling of the wish fulfilled. He believed that whatever you feel yourself to be, you are. Every feeling creates a subconscious impression upon the body and upon your awareness. He knew that a change of feeling is a change of destiny.

I Reached the End of My Rope

Alan had both cancer and Alzheimer's, which made it a very dark period for me. Supporting him through all of his treatments was more than a full time job, and we did not yet have any help in the house. I never had a day off. I was becoming more and more run down and emotionally exhausted. I found a journal from that period where I wrote, "Sometimes I don't want him to get better physically because I'm afraid that his mind won't improve alongside it." I was terrified of the Alzheimer's but had to focus on the cancer.

In my mind's eye, I began to see my mother who took care of my father through a heart attack, prostate cancer, and Alzheimer's for more than twenty years and barely survived. I was following in her footsteps, and this terrified me. Headaches and anxiety plagued me, and I realized that my life as it existed was not sustainable. I saw the long haul ahead of me and wanted to quit—but that wasn't a choice. I felt pressured by knowing that if I didn't take care of Alan to the best of my ability, his symptoms would worsen and he would die an earlier death. Part of me wanted him to die so I could be alleviated of this horrendous task. I even asked myself, "To what extent am I responsible for him?

In my mind, I heard my mother say, "Take care of yourself, Phyllis."

I prayed for guidance and intervention. "Mother Earth and Father Sky, lend me your strength and the power of your partnership to help steer me toward clarity. I want to survive. And I want Alan to live a more quality life. Lift me up by lifting the headaches and letting them go back into the innards of the earth."

Dealing with both cancer and Alzheimer's, Alan lacked the ability to say even a small thank you to me. I saw his profound suffering, but I still wanted him to express some appreciation and not to forget the last twenty-five good years that we had together. I was filled with sadness.

Somewhere inside, I began to see that I was victim of my own mind and that I had some choices. Although I was in a deep state of despair and exhaustion, I knew that I had the resources to get through this. I began to understand that there was deep learning going on inside of me in the midst of my anxiety.

I Asked for Help

One day I woke up and could not stop crying. As is true for many of us, I had a difficult time asking for help, but now, I knew I had to. I was desperate. That is when I called my dear friend, sobbing, and said, "Rachel, I don't think I'm going to make it to the end of the day. I need help."

A couple of days later, we assembled two more friends, and the four of us brainstormed solutions. Rachel had heard about a Care Calendar (CareCalendar.org). We sent an email to many people, explaining the types of support Alan and I needed, and asked them to fill in times in the Care Calendar when they could help. It was as if a miracle occurred overnight. I wept seeing the filled in schedule the following morning. So many people signed up to help us.

The Care Calendar continued for months, until we began to hire caregivers. At first we asked for support two or three times a week, for our helpers to take Alan to medical appointments, or to help with Alan's meals and supplements. During these times, I could rest or take a walk. When I became more exhausted and anxious, we increased the Care Calendar to most days of the week.

I felt scared and vulnerable asking people to help us almost every day, but the response was stunning. It felt miraculous. In addition to personal friends, we had our Center for Spiritual Living community to draw on, and people we did not even know agreed to be part of the team. One such person took Alan to many of his medical appointments, and became a friend over time. Another couple showed up almost weekly to help with whatever we needed. A friend's husband signed up, though we had never met him. Other people agreed to help me grocery shop and run errands. One friend brought a healthy meat dish to us weekly. Another shoveled snow for us. Alan's sister generously came to stay with us for one month, which lightened the need for the Care Calendar. During that time, another friend took me away for five days so I could relax. People gifted Alan with Reiki, chiropractics, EFT (Emotional Freedom Technique), massage, and hypnotherapy sessions, and even gifted me with haircuts and massage. These people felt like angels, who just kept appearing.

The experience was overwhelming and, from it, I learned several important lessons. One is that none of this happened until I asked for help. The universe was not going to read my mind. Even friends did not know exactly what they could do to be useful. I had to ask, to make clear what I needed. People care, but they may not know how to express their care and kindness until you ask. There is deep truth in the saying, "Ask and you shall receive." And once I did ask, I had to surrender to the energy that was larger than myself, this cornucopia of kindness pouring out to Alan and me.

Also, I learned the power of collective effort. There was energy in the community that was greater than the sum of the beautiful individuals who rose up to help. Help did not have to come from any particular person. It was okay that we didn't live near our biological families. It was the emotion, the energetic vibration that mattered. We received huge amounts of love and kindness, and some of it came from strangers. I learned on a deep level that Love Is. Kindness Is. Love comes through a live human being and goes out to others. Our lives were changed because of the love and kindness that came our way.

The Rest of the Story

We returned to the surgeon's office on April 10, 2012. The surgeon examined Alan exactly the way Alan had imagined. At the end of his examination, he said the words that Alan had been visualizing: "I can find no cancer, and the HPV viral wart is gone too."

We embraced and cried in the doctor's office. The alternative modalities worked! Both of us felt the rush of relief and gratitude that Alan had been visualizing.

We were full of joy! We went forward with our plan to celebrate our good news, this healing, with our community of friends in June 2012. There were about 130 people in the room, and it was so quiet that you could hear a pin drop as people listened to every word that Alan and I shared about how he healed from cancer.

We thought that, because the cancer was gone, we might have another year or two of quality living together. But this was not to be. After about six weeks, it became obvious that Alan's Alzheimer's was becoming more pronounced. When we realized this, we felt deep despair and spent much of that week hugging and crying. The Alzheimer's was getting worse. As it turned out, by a rather amazing coincidence, it was exactly one year to the day after he was pronounced free from cancer that Alan began his VSED fast.

CHAPTER SIX
My Personal Journey Through Grief:
Overcoming My Fear of Death

Fear of Death

I want to describe my journey though grief because, as I shall relate, by the end of it, I also found that I was miraculously free of the fear of death that had plagued me for my entire life.

My fear of death began as far back as my memory goes. I knew that my mother was going to leave me someday, that she would die. I was terrified. When I was very young, I used to stand at a window in the house, stare outside, and wonder when my mother would come home. As a young girl, I thought, "If she is going to die and leave me, was I going to die too?" That fear of losing her lasted until her death when she was ninety-five and I was fifty-five. I can remember when she was on her deathbed, and I was in a room nearby, and I spontaneously yelled out, "Please don't leave me." I grieved her death for about four years.

I knew this wasn't healthy behavior for a full-grown adult, so I began to investigate my fear of losing my mother, which led me to investigate my unusual fear of death in general—starting with the fear of my own death. After Alan retired from being a computer consultant, he became an NLP (Neuro-Linguistic Programming) practitioner. NLP has to do with self-limiting beliefs and how those beliefs are often instilled when we are very young through the way we use language. When Alan did

NLP sessions with me, I always ended up at the same place—fear of my own death.

When Alan received the diagnoses of both Alzheimer's and cancer in 2011, I began to come face to face with another roaring fear—feeling alone in the world. I experienced tremendous anxiety and many sleepless nights. My biggest nightmare was actually going to occur. From the time I was seventeen years old, I always had a partner by my side. Alan and I partnered in most of the things that we did, in both business and our personal life for twenty-six years. Like many married couples, we became like one person. I used to envision that we would both live to be old and that he would die first because he was ten years older. Then a few years later, I would die.

Alan's death became a form of death for me. My life changed dramatically. I could not imagine a rebirth for myself. I had no partner, and there were no family members living near me. I was terrified. I was going to be alone in the world with no one to protect me. Some of the pain I was feeling were pains of giving birth to myself, but I didn't know it at the time. I just felt the pain.

The First Few Weeks

Anticipating my new life, living alone, I had carefully planned some activities for the first three weeks after Alan died. Borrowing from Jewish, Buddhist, and Pagan paths, I planned rituals that I knew would be the beginning of my journey through grief. These rituals helped me during the first few weeks, and the memory of them shepherded me through the painful months that were to follow. I mentioned everything I was planning to Alan before he died to obtain his approval. He responded the same way every time: "I don't care what you do. Do whatever you want. I'm not going to be here." His only suggestion was that I put some of his cremated ashes near where our cat is buried. He said, "Then you can visit us both at the same time!" This I did do.

Many years ago, I had read *The Tibetan Book of Living and Dying*, which said that it takes three days for the soul to leave the body. When I read that, I decided that I wanted my own body to be on ice for three days after I died, and I noted this in my Health Directive. Now, I wanted to honor Alan in the same way. First, right after he died, my friend, who was one of the caregivers, and I washed his body. We both noticed how he changed after he died. He looked beautiful. Then, we placed Alan's body on dry ice on a massage table we had prepared ahead of time with draped cloths. It began a three-day vigil during which time someone watched over him all the time, people taking different shifts.

I had invited a death doula, or death midwife, to facilitate our vigil. Death doulas help dying people with individualized care that caters to their physical, mental, emotional, spiritual, and cultural needs. Doulas are not medical people but provide support to help a dying person to have a more conscious, deliberate death. Our death doula was also a personal friend. She follows Pagan rites that have some similarity to those of Tibetan Buddhists. She explained that the spirit slips out quickly, but the trails of residual energy follow slowly behind. These multi-faceted energetic trails are like streamers of multi-colored light containing all the data, information, memoires, and experiences brought into the body over a lifetime and had been stored in the body's cells and energy systems. They merge into the spirit of the deceased and then join into Oneness or God consciousness or the Divine Spirit.

Our death doula explained that our bodies are a collection of five elements: water; earth, as minerals in our cells and bones; fire, represented as electrical energy; and air, including our necessary gases such as oxygen. The fifth sacred element is spirit, that which animates the whole being. When we die, the elements break apart. Fire is the first to depart. Then air leaves the body when the breath stops. Then the spirit leaves. Finally, the body begins to break down as earth and water deconstruct into simple parts and decompose. She explained that these separate elements are then allowed to be resourced back into the whole of existence and to reform in a new collection of elements that will manifest as some new thing. Thus, the cycle of life continues.

The death doula said she could see when the elements left the body. She said that Alan's breakdown occurred perfectly. She was able to witness the final passing of the energy out of his body after watching the energy diminish hourly within and around his body. It was a sweet and quiet observation. There was no drama, just silence and witnessing.

Although I couldn't understand fully, or witness what I was told about the elements leaving the body, I liked the idea of incorporating these rituals. And I liked the idea of having Alan's body in the house for three days so that I could begin to integrate and accept that *he* was no longer in it. His body looked different after he died. He looked gorgeous, younger, relaxed. Right after he died, my caregiver-friend had put a tie around his face to keep his mouth closed until rigor mortis set in; then we could remove it. I continued to kiss him.

These three days also were the first three of seven days of "sitting shiva," a Jewish custom that is a time for friends and family to honor the dead person and to offer support to the grieving family, although the body is usually not present in the Jewish tradition. My dear rabbi friend came every day at 3:00 p.m. and stayed until 7:00 p.m. Anyone who wanted to join us was invited, and many people came. For the first three of the seven days, while his body was still with us, we gathered around Alan. I shared stories about him and our life together, and others joined in with their own stories. There was laughter and there were tears. Friends brought food to share. About one hundred people came through the house that week for sitting shiva.

Once sitting shiva ended, my daughter arrived from Europe and stayed with me for two weeks. She took care of me, did the cooking, ran errands, and brought her smile and good cheer to the house. Alan was her stepdad and she loved him very much. I needed to make physical changes to aide in my transition, so together, my daughter and I boxed up Alan's clothes, and she took them to an agency that provides clothes to needy families.

The Months that Followed

Within months of Alan's death, a friend emailed me a quote by the 17th Century samurai poet Mizuta Masahide: "My barn burned down. Now I can see the moon." I knew it to be a truism, but didn't yet know what I was going to be able to "see" that I couldn't see at the time. My vision was blurred, but I trusted that it would become clear again. I put this quote on the wall close to my desk, along with other inspirational quotes, so I could see them when I needed guidance.

Alan was not the only person whose death I had managed. My active, wise, beloved mother lived with Alan and me for eleven years and died in our home at the age of 95, eleven years before Alan died. She and I talked openly about her death, both jokingly and seriously. At that time, I was consumed with reading about death and dying, including books about eastern philosophy and spirituality, books by Steven Levine and Elisabeth Kubler-Ross, and more. I kept reading until I was satiated with the topic. Much to my surprise, I felt peaceful reading those books. I read excerpts to my mother, and she said multiple times that she had no fear of dying. That was not true for me.

After my mother died, and throughout Alan's illness and VSED preparation, I became increasingly aware that if I didn't face my fear of death, I would never be genuinely free, and I would continue to suffer.

In my twenties, I had read the transcendentalists, such as Emerson and Thoreau. I learned from Ralph Waldo Emerson that, "God will not have his work made manifest by cowards." I knew I had to walk in the direction of my fear and see where it led me, and that the only way to get out of my fear was to go through it. In his essay entitled "Compensation," Emerson said this:

> A fever, a mutilation, a cruel disappointment, a loss of wealth, a loss of friends, seems at the moment unpaid loss, and unpayable. But the sure years reveal the deep remedial force that underlies all facts. The death of a dear friend, wife, brother, lover, which seemed nothing but privation, somewhat later assumes the aspect of a guide or genius; for it commonly operates revolutions in our way of life, terminates an epoch... or a style of living, and allows the formation of new ones, more friendly to the growth of character.

It was not easy to implement the teachings from people I respected such as Pema Chodron, Ralph Waldo Emerson, and my other spiritual teachers. It required great courage on my part. First I had to allow myself to feel deep emotional pain until it went away on its own. I decided I wasn't going to cover it up with external distractions. I wasn't going to camouflage it. I wasn't going to take medication for anxiety. I wasn't going to throw myself into a lot of busy activity. I was just going to stay present to whatever came up.

However, none of the books I had read or the teachings I had tried to follow prepared me in the least for how I truly felt after Alan died. I became a wounded animal, in pain. I couldn't sit still or focus on any activity. I wandered around the house. I called out to Alan, "Hellllloooooo." It took me many months to be able to sit and eat a meal alone in my house without getting up repeatedly. I was aware that I still suffered trauma from the negative backlash I had received from some people in our community, including our hospice. I couldn't go into big public stores with bright lights for at least two months. People ran errands for me. I continued with therapy, but nothing eased the unbearable pain. Many times each day, I would fold over with pain in my heart area and sternum, sobbing, missing my husband. When I was in public, which was limited, and someone asked me how I was doing, I began to cry immediately. I didn't want people to hug me unless they knew me well. It felt invasive.

When I listened to CDs and read books by Pema Chodron, I knew that my life had fallen apart, and that I was responding in a healthy fashion. Her knowledge and words made me feel very human, knowing I was normal and clearly in touch with something very real and difficult in my life. I continued attending the Center for Spiritual Living. Many people in that loving community knew Alan and me well. For close to two years, as soon as I walked in the door of the sanctuary, I dissolved into tears. It was a safe place for me to be with others. Someone's comforting warm embrace was always nearby. No words were needed. This community understood.

Prior to Alan's illnesses, and throughout and after his death, I also found refuge in my daily practices of yoga, meditation, and a walk in the nearby forest. These practices, which I had begun many years earlier, helped to keep me afloat. When I couldn't sleep in the middle of the night, I sat on my cushion and meditated. Then I was able to get back to sleep. After Alan died, my sleep improved because I was no longer dealing with the uncertainty of his death.

I kept a list of friends' names by my desk. When I felt horribly alone and emotionally paralyzed, I looked at my list for someone to call. I had one friend who often met me for a walk and was willing to listen to my tears and angst.

I continued to experience and watch the grief. It moved through me organically, and had a life of its own. I didn't judge the grief. I didn't do anything to make it go away. I never felt there was anything wrong with me. I didn't judge myself and think it was taking me too long to get over the grief or tell myself I had to get over it in a particular period of time. Nevertheless, it was the most devastating emotional pain I've ever experienced, and I couldn't see beyond it.

I spent much of my time alone, and felt very lonely. I would have liked it if more people had understood how difficult it was for me to go home alone and had invited me to their homes for dinner or to join them at a movie. This occurred rarely. I understood that most people didn't know how to act around me and that they were uncomfortable with issues around illness and death. Perhaps I brought up their own fears of what could happen to them. In any case, they had no idea how to console me. It would have been easier for me if I had worn black for one year to symbolize that I was grieving. In the appendices, you will find some guidelines about how to be around people who are grieving.

Finding Grief Support

I knew I needed grief support. I continued seeing my therapist every week or two, but I felt I needed to be around people who were experiencing grief from losing a husband. I didn't know where to turn. We have some grief support in our town but it is more of a drop-in situation. Also, our local grief support is facilitated mostly by our local hospice. Our hospice had turned their back on Alan and me, so how could I feel supported there? If anything, my grief and despair was augmented by our local hospice and others who were critical of Alan's decision.

By this time, I had become friends with the volunteer chaplain from End of Life Washington, the person who had told me about VSED in the first place. The first time I called this loving woman, she listened to me cry over the phone for about an hour. At the end of the call, she said, "I'm going to visit my elderly mother in Kansas soon. I'm going to give you my cell phone number. I want you to know that you can call me anytime." I believed her and was overwhelmed with her kindness. I did call her when I needed to. After about five phone conversations, we realized that we liked one another, and we decided to meet in person. We both drove about an hour and met at a park one afternoon. We have become dear friends.

One day, about a year after Alan died, we were visiting and I began to tell her about the lack of local grief support in our town. I don't remember who suggested it first, but she said she would facilitate a grief support group if I found the people. I quickly went to work and found five other women interested in the subject. Five of the six of us had husbands who had died recently. This was my first opportunity to truly understand that I was not alone. There were others who were experiencing the depth of pain and anguish that I was feeling. Sharing this experience, together in community, was a step toward healing my broken heart.

Gradual Recovery

After one year, I noticed I was crying less often, and that my tears were not as painful. I kept crying until I didn't need to cry anymore. The grief lifted little by little and I began to leave the house more often, see friends, watch movies, and visit my family in Europe. Eventually, I felt lighter.

I remember the first time I felt joy again. It was about two-and-a-half years after Alan died. I was standing at my kitchen sink washing dishes and looking outside at other houses and trees. I was very present. Then I realized that for no specific reason, I felt joyous. It was not attached to an activity, or even a thought that was occurring in my imagination. It was just there. It was more than feeling peaceful. There was an overall calm, an energetic feeling, an opening in my heart and solar plexus. I felt content for no particular reason. I didn't need anything. I wasn't thinking about the future or the past.

I used to think of happiness as the result of an event, but I was now learning that joy is pure and resides inside of me for no particular reason. This was a stunning experience for me, a powerful lesson. After that, joy began to occur spontaneously, regardless of my activity. I never knew when this new friend would pop up inside me. She began to visit more often. I began to notice that I wasn't feeling anxious. It was as though I was growing a new person inside of me. These occurrences of spontaneous joy and being able to feel more comfortable alone in the house, in my own skin, continued. I noticed and appreciated these feelings whenever they arose.

I began to truly hear the sweet song of birds at daybreak. I began to hear the rustle in the trees. One day, I realized that I had stopped feeling uncomfortable around couples who were happily married. I became grateful for each day of life. I began to approach every day as if it may be my last. For quite a while, I put a note on the floor by my bed that said, "Is this the day I'm going to die?" It was a good reminder about presence. My appreciation of stillness and silence continued to grow.

My heart broke and, in its breaking, I began to hold more love than I've ever held before, not for particular people, but for Life. I was experiencing what Hazrat Inayat Khan meant when he said, "God breaks the heart again and again and again until it stays open." My heart flowered and opened. I have a connection with all of Life, with all people, with each encounter. All my senses have been enlivened. And this connection is not only with those I see and feel and hear and touch; it continues with Alan. He is still with me. I can hear his words, feel his presence, know his eternal love. All that really changed is that he left his body, and our relationship has been rearranged.

I noticed that I became more generous and wanted to help others more. I became proud of my inner growth and my strengths, and I forgave my weaknesses. As I began to let go of fears, I began to feel free inside, and with this newfound freedom, I gradually discovered that I was no longer afraid to die.

I know that a big piece of my healing was my decision to share Alan's and my story publicly, and my commitment to spread information about VSED and expanding choices about how and when we die. It was true that Alan had requested that he wanted "everyone to know about VSED," and that I always was aware that I told him, "You'll just have to trust that I'll be your vehicle." Yet, in an even bigger way, I am doing this work for myself, because I know I have an unusual opportunity to help others who are in similar situations. I'm doing it because I know I'm no different from any other human. We all have the capacity to love and to grieve. And I have learned that by helping others, I am helping myself; the love and self-understanding come right back to me. I have felt the same need and commitment to share our story that

I had when I was committed to helping Alan have a good quality death. It is something I feel called to do.

I gave my TEDx talk only seven months after Alan died. After that, I've had a steady stream of presentations and interviews. This felt meaningful and natural. It continues to this day, and it remains a major component in my healing from grief and my ability to move forward with my life. I created a website to assist others with information (www. PhyllisShacter.com), and I hope this book will add more depth and reach those who might not ever see my website.

Connecting with Others

Three-and-a-half years after Alan died, I still had never met anyone whose spouse died by going through the VSED process. I was alone in this way. Then one day, I heard about a man whose wife had died about four months earlier using VSED, and that they had learned about VSED from me when I gave a local presentation! Through networking, I was able to obtain his contact information and invited him over for a meal. He could barely get in the front door before we began to ask each other many questions about our VSED experiences. Although the details of our stories were different, the connection with someone who had had this common experience was enormously comforting, and I realized that, whether I know them or not, many other people will have their own VSED experience, just as we did. Our animated conversation helped me feel more connected to my human family.

The Death of My Fear of Death

I am now free of the fear of death that so burdened much of my life, and I truly feel like an entirely new person. If I could help others release their fear of death, this would make me so very happy. It's a journey each person must take individually. No one can do the work or take the journey for you. But I hope sharing my story will help.

For many years, my fear of my own death was inextricably bound up with my fear of the death of my mother and then of my husband. I was emotionally paralyzed when I couldn't imagine life without them. Now they have both died, and I have survived. Not only am I alive, I am living with a great deal of joyous gratitude, a deep sense of self-reliance, and interdependence with others.

My fear of death is gone. Where did it go?

Though I did not realize it at the time, my experience of grief, over my mother's and my husband's deaths, was extreme partly because I was grieving my own death at the same time. My fear of being left alone was, in part, my fear of having no one around me as I aged and died. As my grief over my terrible losses began to ebb, so did my fear of death in general, and specifically, my own death.

It definitely helped me to see them both die in great peace and with no fear. Both of them even had curiosity about what it would be like to die and what would come next. This made an impression on me. Whenever I thought about death, I felt like I was suffocating and being annihilated, which truly frightened me.

My willingness to experience my grief fully is precisely what allowed me to finally be free of it. If I had tried to pretend the pain was not there, busied myself so I wouldn't have to feel it, kept myself distracted, or covered it up with false "happiness," it would still be there, beneath the surface, keeping me a slave to the cover ups so I would not have to feel it. Only by experiencing the pain and surviving, could I, in the end, be truly free of it. And the unexpected gift, as I emerged on the other side of my painful despair, was the gift of accepting that I am going to die and that this is okay. This is Alan's most important legacy to me. To live without the underlying fear of death is like being a bird in flight. I am free.

Another piece of Alan's legacy is that I don't feel he went anywhere. What died? His body? He is still inside me as alive as ever. Regardless of how my personal life evolves, Alan's love is permanent, eternal.

Alan figured out a way to redirect his life through VSED. I'm redirecting and recreating my life daily, knowing that I have little control over what occurs. I live with more presence and trust in Life and Love than ever before.

I know I'm going to leave this body. Even if I live for another twenty or thirty years, it doesn't seem far off. I live each day preparing myself to die by being present to what I'm doing now. I'm okay with not having any definite answers. I'm living with a strong foundation of inner growth and gratitude for the gift of life today. I believe that how I live my life will affect the way I die. The poet Rilke said, to paraphrase, that death is not the scissors that cut off the rope of life at the end; death is one of the strands woven into the rope of life.

Close to three years after Alan died, I had a profound dream. I always keep paper and pen next to my bed to help me recall dreams. When I awoke in the morning, I saw a paper on the floor. I had written the following: "I overdosed and died. Peace." To this day I remember that feeling of deep peace even though I was dead (in my dream). That dream was a turning point in my life because, though I was feeling freer already, it offered an actual *experience* of the peacefulness that death can be. It is not suffocation and annihilation at all. It is the next natural thing that happens after life, an easy, peaceful transition to whatever lies beyond. The remembrance of this dream and the sensation I felt was in deep contrast to the way I felt for most of my life. That peace is now deep within me.

I believe my suffering contained the seed for my growth and evolution. My experience of growing beyond my deep grief actually rewrote the genetic code within my cellular matter and that even my biochemistry has changed. I feel like a new person. Instead of being focused on my limitations, I see my strengths and gifts. My heart is open toward my limitations and the limitations of others. This all occurred naturally because I was willing to face my deepest fears.

Poetry captures essence so beautifully. I came across this poem by D.H. Lawrence in recent months. It captures my life today.

Go deeper than love, for the soul has greater depths,
Love is like the grass, but the heart is deep wild rock,
   Molten, yet dense and permanent.
Go deep to your deep old heart, and lose sight of yourself,
   And lose sight of me, the me whom you turbulently loved.
   Let us lose sight of ourselves, and break the mirrors.
For the fierce curve of our lives is moving again to the depths
   Out of sight, in the deep living heart.

APPENDIX I
Medical Resources and Checklists

What follows is necessary medical preparation for the caregivers and family of any person preparing to VSED.

1. Obtain Medical Support for the VSED Process

A doctor or nurse practitioner comfortable with end-of-life care is an essential part of any VSED team, so that the patient can be monitored and kept comfortable. Hunger is not usually a problem, but dehydration can become uncomfortable, and there can be side effects, including delirium. A doctor can sedate the patient to a level of comfort.

Hospice doctors are ideal. If you or your loved one is planning to VSED, check with your local hospice to find out if they will support you. Apparently there is no standardized policy from hospice regarding VSED support. Hospices affiliated with religious organizations may decline to assist.

Hospice is an ideal support system if it is available to you because they are experts in end-of-life care; they offer necessary equipment, supplies, and medications; and they provide both medical supervision and social work services. Without hospice, you will need to pull together a private team. Even if the patient is in hospice, you may want to obtain additional caregiving help.

If you are in hospice, you may prefer to go through the VSED process in your own home. It can become complicated if you have to contend with the beliefs of a variety of staff in a hospice house setting.

If your hospice will not support VSED, find a private doctor or nurse practitioner who will provide medical supervision and medication. Most doctors are not set up to make house calls during the day or be available twenty-four hours by phone, yet both of those kinds of support are very helpful. Find a doctor or service that can provide them.

2. Hire Appropriate Caregivers

Most caregivers are trained to help people prolong life rather than to support an elective death, so it can be a challenge to find the right professional caregivers who will understand and support VSED. Your caregiver must be genuinely respectful of the patient's and family's choice while providing expert physical care. Based on my experience, it's necessary to have twenty-four hour professional caregiving support.

To help care for Alan, I hired two Certified Nursing Assistants on twelve-hour shifts. Three professionals on eight-hour shifts would also have worked well. As the VSED progressed, the CNA's found that they appreciated the continuity that the two of them provided. I found these two women through personal networking, but agencies are available in most towns.

Friends and family may not be ideal caregivers because they lack critical skills such as turning a person in bed, applying an adult diaper, administering a suppository, preventing bedsores, keeping the face moistened, bathing the body, and more. Also, they may think they are doing the patient a favor by supplying small sips of water or juice. This is no favor to the patient, as it will prolong the dying process.

3. Consider Using a Death Doula

There is a small but growing movement of death doulas or death midwives. These people can help to manage a VSED case and stay in close contact with the doctor. To find one and to learn more about what they do, go to the website of the International End of Life Doula Association. www.inelda.org

4. Obtain All Supplies Ahead of Time

Both the caregivers and the VSED patient will be very grateful to have the following supplies ready to go on the day the VSED fast begins. If you have the support of your local hospice, they will be able to supply these items. Otherwise, you can purchase them at medical supply stores or regular pharmacies.

- Eye drops, lip balm, and body lotion. You will administer these routinely to soothe eyes, lips, and skin.
- Small one-ounce spray bottles. Be sure they spray only fine mist. These are essential to moisten a dry mouth but provide minimal hydration (they do not quench thirst).
- Disposable oral swab sticks. These are little sponges on a stick, good for cleaning the teeth, gums, and tongue. They should not be used to deliver moisture for two reasons: First, the sponge can hold too much water and interfere with the goal of withholding fluids. Second, the patient might reflexively chomp down on the stick and could potentially bite the sponge portion off, creating a choking hazard.
- Tab-style adult diapers. These are to be used when a person can no longer get out of bed. They can be used

open under the person, or tabbed closed.

- Bedpan to be used if a person is conscious and needs to eliminate but can no longer get up.
- Hand held urinal for men, easier than a bedpan if the need to void is felt.
- Three or four cloth reusable waterproof pads, also referred to as draw sheets. These come in various sizes but no smaller than 30" x 34." They are placed under the person in bed. Besides protecting the bed from fluids, they are essential for moving the person easily and comfortably.
- Disposable waterproof rectangular under-pads used on top of draw sheets and also on furniture if the person is sitting up out of bed.
- Wash cloths, hand towels, and baby wipes.
- Disposable gloves are available in latex or non-latex.
- Large plastic garbage bags for used adult diapers, baby wipes, etc.
- Bell for patient to ring for help.
- A cool mist humidifier will provide moisture in the air and help offset the bodily drying sensations brought on by dehydration
- A bedside commode is useful when a person can no longer get to the bathroom but is able to get up independently or with assist.
- A hospital bed helps the caregivers to provide better care as the process continues. The bed can be raised to provide easier care access; lowered so the patient can get out of bed more easily; and raised and lowered at head and foot to vary body position, make the patient more comfortable, and prevent pressure sores. The ability to raise the head of the bed can become important at later stages as breathing and lung clarity changes, and is necessary when administering medication.
- A gait belt is worn around the patient's waist, which

allows a caregiver to hold, guide, and stabilize the person without risk of injury caused from holding on to the arm or clothing. If you hire professional caregivers, they will likely bring a gait belt, so check with them before purchasing one.

- A & D Ointment, or some other moisture barrier cream. This can be helpful in hip creases, inner thighs, and buttock region for moisture or friction aggravation.
- A baby monitor will enable you to listen for the person's needs when you are not in the room with him or her.

Summary Shopping Lists
From the Drugstore
Eye Drops
Lip Balm
Body Lotion
Small Spray Bottle
Disposable Oral Swab Sticks
Tab Style Diapers
Reusable Waterproof Pads (Draw Sheets)
Disposable Waterproof Rectangular Under Pads
Handheld Urinal for Men
Bed Pan
A & D Ointment
Baby Wipes
Disposable Gloves
Garbage Bags

From Medical Supply Store
Gait Belt
Hospital Bed
Bedside Commode

5. Prepare the Patient
Alan had a clear marker so he would know when it was time to start the VSED process. This is essential. Also, five days prior to starting the VSED process, Alan chose

to reduce his calorie intake to about 500 calories per day. This may have helped speed up the VSED process. His body was healthy, and he wanted to die and go through the VSED process as quickly as possible. A person can go without food for many days, but for far less time without water. If a person is very overweight, it may take him or her longer to VSED. You can discuss this issue with your doctor.

6. VSED in a Dementia Facility

If a patient with a neurological disease is in a health facility and has completed a Health Directive in advance, specifying that the health agent has the power to request that food and water be withheld when the diseased person can no longer feed him or herself, it is still unlikely that the facility will cooperate because of the fear of legal liability. Also, revolving staff members may not understand, or in some cases even agree with VSED, so the person's support will be inconsistent. Hopefully, health facilities will become more supportive in the future.

7. The Patient is in Charge

Remember that the person going through the VSED process is ultimately in charge, and is allowed to change his or her mind. If the decision has been made with great care and thoughtfulness, and the patient is kept comfortable with appropriate medication, this is not likely to happen.

APPENDIX II
Legal Resources and Documents

VSED is a legal option. The U.S. Supreme Court in 1997 ruled that anyone may refuse lifesaving medical treatment. It has also asserted that anyone may refuse food and hydration. Nevertheless, Alan and I wanted to be thorough in our effort to protect ourselves and everyone who was involved with us. We hired an elder care attorney and followed her recommendations. It was our experience that our elder care attorney knew more about end-of-life matters than most estate planning attorneys.

This Appendix lists resources and documents that we found useful and that I recommend. As I related in the book, we had a most unexpected visit from an Adult Protective Services social worker. She was impressed with the legal documents and information that I was able to produce.

Legal Resources
1. End of Life Washington
The organization's comprehensive website provides explanations of and templates for numerous legal documents. You will have to see if you can use their documents in your state, but they at least offer an excellent education about the general range of documents available. www.endoflifewa.org

2. Compassion and Choices
This is a national organization with offices in several states. They lobby for just end-of life-legislation, and they provide a wealth of information, support, and referrals. Especially if you are not able to engage hospice for support, Compassion and Choices will be able to provide guidance and referrals. www.compassionandchoices.org

3. A Legal Opinion
A thorough, in-depth legal opinion about Voluntarily Stopping Eating and Drinking can be found in the article by Thaddeus Pope and Lindsey Anderson entitled "Voluntarily Stopping Eating and Drinking: A Legal Treatment Option at the End of Life." I printed this article and kept it handy in case others wanted to see it. https://papers.ssrn.com/sol3/papers.cfm?abstract_id=1689049

4. A Values Work Sheet
The End of Life Washington website offers a Values Work Sheet. We found it useful to help us clarify our needs and desires.

5. Other Websites
Several other websites have useful information about VSED and end-of-life matters. Remember that some states have special requirements and laws, so consulting an elder care attorney may be an excellent idea.

Honing the Emerging Right to Stop Eating and Drinking. http://blogs.harvard.edu/billofhealth/2016/11/18/patients-right-to-stop-eating-and-drinking/

Can the Right to Stop Eating and Drinking be Exercised via a Surrogate Acting Pursuant to an Advanced Instruction? http://blogs.harvard.edu/billofhealth/2017/01/23/can-the-right-to-sed-be-exercised-via-a-surrogate-acting-pursuant-to-an-advance-instruction/ #more-20582

Five Wishes. www.agingwithdignity.org/five-wishes/about-five-wishes

Phyllis Shacter offers a lot of information on her site. www.phyllisshacter.com

Legal Documents

The following legal documents are useful in two ways: First, they give you legal protection and confidence that you will be properly represented by your health agents. Second, the process of preparing the documents encourages you to think through the philosophical, ethical, and practical nuances involved with VSED. The documents raise provocative questions and provide a background for important conversations among the loved ones involved.

1. The Health Directive

It is an excellent idea to complete an Advance Health Care Directive, sometimes called a Living Will, while you are healthy and mentally competent, long in advance of the time you might need it. This document states clearly your desires for your care if you become unable to make decisions for yourself.

The comprehensive template for a Health Directive on the End of Life Washington website makes it manageable to create this valuable document for yourself. The final document has to be witnessed and notarized. I believe everyone over eighteen years old should have one. If you do not have a Health Directive, usually a default surrogate will make the decisions for you. Almost every state has a list that starts with the spouse and then the adult child. As part of the Directive, assign at least two health agents to represent you if you can't represent yourself. If you do not choose who makes decisions for you, the person who ends up doing it may not the person who knows you or cares about you. It is useful to think about all of the options the document presents, all of the what-ifs, long before you are in a position to need them, and to discuss all of your choices with your health agents every year or two.

I keep copies of my health directive in the following places:

- Each of my health agents
- My local primary care doctor
- My local hospital records department
- The glove compartment of my car
- My suitcase when I travel
- With my financial advisor
- On the front of my refrigerator, next to a POLST form (see below)

2. The Alzheimer's Disease/Dementia Mental Health Advance Directive

This form is similar to an Advance Health Directive but is specifically for Alzheimer's and other dementia-related illnesses. It allows people coping with Alzheimer's disease and dementia to document their wishes about the specific challenges of living with these illnesses. It has to be completed, witnessed, and notarized while the diseased person is still mentally competent. Some people decide to fill this out long before they are diagnosed with any disease.

The End of Life Washington website offers an Alzheimer's Disease/Dementia Mental Health Advance Directive that is legal in Washington (and possibly other states) and in any case, can be used to document your wishes and provide a guide to your family and health care providers. http://endoflifewa.org/alzheimers-diseasedementia-advance-directive

Parts of this Directive may require legal guidance. For example, an important section allows you to set up measures that protect your income and assets, even if you end up living in an expensive dementia facility.

3. Release and Assumption of Risk

Our elder care attorney wrote these two original documents. One was signed over Alan's name, and one was signed over my name. In this document, the person who is going to VSED takes full responsibility for his or her decision, thereby eliminating risk to a spouse, other family members, caregivers, and the doctor.

4. Physician Orders for Life-Sustaining Treatment (POLST)

We used our state's POLST form. The Washington form is neon green and printed on heavy stock that is posted in a prominent place in the home, most often on the refrigerator. The form allows an individual with a serious illness or fragility to summarize his or her wishes regarding life-sustaining treatment. Emergency personnel responding to a call are trained to look for the bright green colored form and to respect the treatment decisions outlined on it. If the form says, "Do not resuscitate," emergency personnel can respect this request without concern for legal repercussions. To be legal, the form must have been signed by both the doctor and the patient at the same time. I keep mine on my refrigerator with a magnet, next to a copy of my Health Directive. Many states offer a form like this one from Washington. It's ideal to create your POLST form while you are still healthy. http://polst/org/programs-in-your-state

5. Durable Power of Attorney

This form assigns to a specific person of your choosing the legal power to handle your finances when you can no longer do so yourself. Durable Power of Attorney forms are available online, or any attorney can assist you to create one. It is a good form to have on hand, along with your Will and your Health Directive. Create this document long before you think you will need it.

6. A Letter to Your Doctor

You may want to write a letter directly to your primary care doctor stating your end-of-life desires. Good communication with this person is essential. The End of Life Washington website offers several templates for such a letter.

APPENDIX III
How To Help a Grieving Friend:
11 Things to Do When You Are Not Sure What to Do
by Megan Devine
[Originally Published in the *Huffington Post* 10/24/14]
For more useful information on grieving:
www.refugeingrief.com

I've been a therapist for more than 10 years. I worked in social services for the decade before that. I knew grief. I knew how to handle it in myself, and how to attend to it in others. When my partner drowned on a sunny day in 2009, I learned there was a lot more to grief than I'd known.

Many people truly want to help a friend or family member who is experiencing a severe loss. Words often fail us at times like these, leaving us stammering for the right thing to say. Some people are so afraid to say or do the wrong thing, they choose to do nothing at all. Doing nothing at all is certainly an option, but it's not often a good one.

While there is no one perfect way to respond or to support someone you care about, here are some good ground rules.

1. Grief belongs to the griever
You have a supporting role, not the central role, in your friend's grief. This may seem like a strange thing to say. So

many of the suggestions, advice and "help" given to the griever tells them they should be doing this differently, or feeling differently than they do. Grief is a very personal experience, and belongs entirely to the person experiencing it. You may believe you would do things differently if it had happened to you. We hope you do not get the chance to find out. This grief belongs to your friend: follow his or her lead.

2. Stay present and state the truth

It's tempting to make statements about the past or the future when your friend's present life holds so much pain. You cannot know what the future will be, for yourself or your friend—it may or may not be better "later." That your friend's life was good in the past is not a fair trade for the pain of now. Stay present with your friend, even when the present is full of pain.

It's also tempting to make generalized statements about the situation in an attempt to soothe your friend. You cannot know that your friend's loved one "finished their work here," or that they are in a "better place." These future-based, omniscient, generalized platitudes aren't helpful. Stick with the truth: this hurts. I love you. I'm here.

3. Do not try to fix the unfixable

Your friend's loss cannot be fixed or repaired or solved. The pain itself cannot be made better. Please see #2. Do not say anything that tries to fix the unfixable, and you will do just fine. It is an unfathomable relief to have a friend who does not try to take the pain away.

4. Be willing to witness searing, unbearable pain

To do number four while also practicing number three is very, very hard.

5. This is not about you

Being with someone in pain is not easy. You will have things come up—stresses, questions, anger, fear, guilt. Your feelings will likely be hurt. You may feel ignored and unappreciated. Your friend cannot show up for their part of the relationship very well. Please don't take it personally, and please don't take it out on them. Please find your own people to lean on at this time—it's important that you be supported while you support your friend. When in doubt, refer to #1.

6. Anticipate, don't ask

Do not say, "Call me if you need anything," because your friend will not call. Not because they do not need, but because identifying a need, figuring out who might fill that need, and then making a phone call to ask is light years beyond their energy levels, capacity, or interest. Instead, make concrete offers: "I will be there at 4 p.m. on Thursday to bring your recycling to the curb," or "I will stop by each morning on my way to work and give the dog a quick walk." Be reliable.

7. Do the recurring things

The actual, heavy, real work of grieving is not something you can do (see #1), but you can lessen the burden of "normal" life requirements for your friend. Are there recurring tasks or chores that you might do? Things like walking the dog, refilling prescriptions, shoveling snow, and bringing in the mail are all good choices. Support your friend in small, ordinary ways—these things are tangible evidence of love. Please try not to do anything that is irreversible—like doing laundry or cleaning up the house—unless you check with your friend first. That empty soda bottle beside the couch may look like trash, but may have been left there by their husband just the other day. The dirty laundry may be the last thing that smells like her. Do you see where I'm going here? Tiny little normal things become precious. Ask first.

8. Tackle projects together
Depending on the circumstance, there may be difficult tasks that need tending—things like casket shopping, mortuary visits, the packing and sorting of rooms or houses. Offer your assistance and follow through with your offers. Follow your friend's lead in these tasks. Your presence alongside them is powerful and important; words are often unnecessary. Remember #4: bear witness and be there.

9. Run interference
To the new griever, the influx of people who want to show their support can be seriously overwhelming. What is an intensely personal and private time can begin to feel like living in a fish bowl. There might be ways you can shield and shelter your friend by setting yourself up as the designated point person—the one who relays information to the outside world, or organizes well-wishers. Gatekeepers are really helpful.

10. Educate and advocate
You may find that other friends, family members, and casual acquaintances ask for information about your friend. You can, in this capacity, be a great educator, albeit subtly. You can normalize grief with responses like, "She has better moments and worse moments and will for quite some time. An intense loss changes every detail of your life." If someone asks you about your friend a little further down the road, you might say things like, "Grief never really stops. It is something you carry with you in different ways."

11. Love

Above all, show your love. Show up. Say something. Do something. Be willing to stand beside the gaping hole that has opened in your friend's life, without flinching or turning away. Be willing to not have any answers. Listen. Be there. Be present. Be a friend. Be love. Love is the thing that lasts.

Megan Devine is the author of Everything is Not Okay: an audio program for grief. *She is a licensed clinical counselor, writer, and grief advocate. You can find her at www.refugeingrief. com. Join her on Facebook at www.facebook.com/refugeingrief*

APPENDIX IV
Our Last Conversation with Alan

On December 12, 2012, my daughter Erica flew over from her home in Belgium so that she and my granddaughter, age twelve, could visit with Alan one last time. We decided to "interview" Alan, and it turned out to be the last substantial conversation any of us had with him. His clarity about what he had learned from life, some of it recently, was quite impressive, considering his state. Some of it was mature spiritual wisdom.

We were upstairs in our spacious den, all snuggled into comfortable chairs, with a resplendent view of Bellingham Bay and the Canadian mountains. I used shorthand to record the conversation. Alan died four months later.

We began by talking to Alan about how he healed naturally from laryngeal cancer in only four months.

Alan: I think the fact that so many people were praying for me daily at 7:30 pm had a huge impact on me. There were hundreds of people who claimed they were praying for me for four months. That's a lot.

A big part of it is accepting the fact that I was going to die. It opened me up for everything else. Maybe I didn't have to pretend anymore. Up to that point, I felt my life was a big pretense, and I was trying to live up to the image that I had of myself, as to what I was supposed to be. And once I got a critical illness, then none of that made a difference anymore.

I was a Harvard graduate. I was a brain. I went through life pleasing other people and always living up to these standards. Then I got cancer, and lost my brain to Alzheimer's. I realized that I'm okay just the way I am. I have inner peace that I've never had before.

It doesn't matter what you do. It only matters how you do it. I always thought it mattered what I did and how I prepared for that, and now I know it doesn't make any difference. Now I know it's how you go about doing it. I learned to accept myself for what I am and not for what I do.

Phyllis and Erica: What are you?

Alan: I am peace. I am love. I am loved. We all have beliefs about what we think we should do and be. A belief is a story you have about yourself. It is not the Truth. I think for me all of my beliefs were limiting. And I've learned to let that go. Maybe someone will read your book and say, "I have a belief about myself and it's not true." If you change your beliefs, you can change your life.

The power of my mind changed my beliefs from having cancer to not having cancer. I imagined daily going back to the surgeon and him examining me and saying, "I no longer see the cancer; and the viral wart is gone too."

I know that I'm going to die soon. There is no fear. In fact, I'm kind of looking forward to it. I'm very curious. In fact, I'm sure that there are other planes of existence. And I'm curious as to what they are, how they are, and how they affect this planet, and maybe other planets.

Phyllis and Erica: How did you get to a place of being fearless? Have you always been fearless?

Alan: No. I don't know how I got there. It just happened. I was scared of dying. I didn't know what was going to happen. But now I'm not afraid. I'm curious.

Phyllis and Erica: You've been a spiritual seeker since the 1960s. What have you done and how has it affected your life today?

Alan: I don't know if I've been a spiritual seeker because I wasn't looking for anything. But I was curious about life and what causes people to do what they do. I've done a lot of meditation of various kinds, of various schools.

Phyllis and Erica: How do you think meditation has helped you?

Alan: It has helped me not get caught up in the insanity that surrounds us all. I think there must be a reason for everything. It seems like life is a big experiment to see what happens. If someone is organizing this existence— I'm assuming this is occurring, some energy is doing it— it's like a big experiment or maybe lots of experiments, and the one I'm in, organized by some energy, is to see what happens to me, the earth, the people who are close to me, people who aren't close to me. I think it's random. My sense is that everyone who comes up to a spiritual path understands a tiny bit of essential truth and is trying to figure it out. But the truth is a huge concept. They experience it differently.

Phyllis and Erica: What did you do to become so accepting of your death?

Alan: Once I knew I had cancer and thought I might die, I suddenly thought it was okay. I can't attribute it to anything I did. Death happens to everyone.

Phyllis and Erica: What did you have to do to get to this point of acceptance?

Alan: As what I can do with my mind decreases, there is less and less stuff that is important or matters.

Phyllis and Erica: What matters now?

Alan: Love and appreciation. My parents were very critical of everything. One day I was at the dinner table and was holding a cup wrong. My father went ballistic. He just got furious with me. How you did things was important to them, and to their friends. They were legitimately worried that I would be in public and hold my cup wrong and disgrace them. And people would say, "Did you see how Alan held his cup?"

One day I came back from camp, age ten or eleven, and my mother turned to me in the middle of the day and said, "This is the first day I can remember in a long time where you didn't do something that you needed to be punished for."

The other experience that informed my life was when I was in the first grade, my father said to me, "You have to do well in the first grade because if you don't, you won't be able to do well in the second grade, the third grade, and on and on." So I was always trying to do better. I was always trying to please my parents. This went on for a long time.

Phyllis and Erica: When did it stop?

Alan: I think fairly recently. I don't even think about what people think about me anymore, and I did for most of my life.

Phyllis and Erica: Did it stop before or after you got cancer?

Alan: It was around the time I got cancer. I knew at that point that I was mortal, and so if I was going to die, it wouldn't make any difference what I did.

Phyllis and Erica: Was the cancer a gift or a curse to you?

Alan: Definitely a gift. Once I realized I was going to die, it didn't make a difference what I did. I think I was open to receiving love. I think I had always assumed that people didn't love me. And then when I got cancer, people started responding and visiting and bringing food and helping, and I realized that they loved me, not for what I did, but because of who I was. In that sense cancer was a big gift. People started treating me differently when I got cancer, and I saw the love behind it.

Phyllis and Erica: How did Science of Mind influence you? *(Alan and I had been attending the Center for Spiritual Living for some years, where we learned the Science of Mind philosophy.)*

Alan: You are what you think. On a different level, NLP (Neuro-Linguistic Programming) is more cerebral. Science of Mind is, you get what you believe. The concept of Spirit isn't involved in NLP. But many premises are the same. God or Spirit is a big part of Science of Mind.

* * *

Alan and I expressed our love and appreciation for one another up to the last day of his life. We were both grateful that he was able to VSED and did not have to live into the late stages of Alzheimer's. He died while he was still capable of experiencing and expressing this beautiful inner peace.

ACKNOWLEDGEMENTS

I give thanks to Susan Page, my sister-in-law, who is an accomplished author, public speaker, and founder and director of the San Miguel Writers' Conference and Literary Festival. Without her help, this book may not have happened. She championed the idea for the book, provided me with outlines to work from, edited and re-wrote information along the way. She referred me to all the perfect publishing and promotion resources. She is a full partner in this book; we birthed it together.

Mayer Shacter, my brother, reinforced his belief in this project by giving his wife Susan all the support and time she needed to help me with the book.

I give my heartfelt love and thanks to Alan's physician, who in this book is referred to as Dr. Dora. She gave compassionate and excellent care to Alan throughout his VSED process. She has been a blessing in our lives. I will always feel deep gratitude for her support and guidance and friendship.

Two close friends, Gloria Harrison and Leslie Powell Shankman, met with me often to brainstorm the development of my website. The book grew out of that website. Gloria saw the vision of this book before I did, and she encouraged me every step of the way.

I met Leslie Powell Shankman soon after I moved to Bellingham in 2004. More than anyone else, she has stood by my side, listened to me, consoled me and has been a loving friend. As a retired professional caregiver, she stepped forward only days before Alan began to VSED, and became part of his caregiving team. She contributed to this book by writing beautifully about what occurred during Alan's nine and a half day passage.

Maymie Dixon was a primary caregiver on our team. She helped Alan and me for five months prior to and throughout his VSED experience. This woman has an open heart, deep integrity, and deep knowledge about her profession. She has become a dear friend.

I am grateful for the professional and thoughtful caregivers who took care of Alan prior to his VSED experience.

Deep thanks go to Rose LaBelle for her support as a dear friend, and for her help orchestrating the community Care Calendar. Rose then turned the Care Calendar over to dear Rabbi Kalish (Marti) Leviel. Thank you Kalish for all your help and for orchestrating the sitting shiva process during the first days of mourning. Rose and Kalish are both treasures.

Deep thanks to Andrea Asebedo, minister of our ever-expanding Center for Spiritual Living community in Bellingham, Washington. She, along with the community supported Alan and me through his illness and dying process. This community is my extended family.

Thank you to April Eberhardt, who gave me early encouragement and referred me to my editor, Terry Persun. From our first conversation, I trusted Terry and appreciated his professionalism. He has been generous, kind and competent every step of the way.

I give thanks to Trudy James, chaplain, and producer of the "Speaking of Dying" film. She is the person who first told me about Voluntarily Stopping Eating and Drinking. She always had time for me when I was grieving and needed to talk. As time went on, we became close friends.

I give thanks to Jenny Macke for being a loving friend to Alan and me, and helping to make arrangements for the three-day vigil which occurred after Alan's death.

Thank you, Ashley Benem, for all your blessings and finding all the people who participated in the three-day vigil following Alan's death. You have been generous and kind.

Thank you, Jandira McCarthy, for spending most of the time during the VSED process at our house, being by my side, taking care of me, consoling me and keeping the caregivers sane.

Thank you, Mary Jensen, for your integrity and showing up consistently to help both Alan and me.

I thank my web designer, Phillip Flores. His skill, friendship, and integrity shine.

I thank Emma Young, my college assistant, for her competence, intelligence, and creativity.

I thank Ryan Shupe who has been a true friend and generously and compassionately has helped me countless times with the computer, never asking for anything in return.

I thank Quinn Cook, my publicist, for arriving at the perfect time with enthusiasm and vision for this book.

More thanks go to Erin Crisman Glass JD who became our elder care attorney. Her kindness and professionalism and knowledge made us feel more comfortable with our decision. She also was one of the original people who worked on the development of the first VSED Conference in October 2016.

I give thanks to Timothy Quill, MD and Thaddeus Pope, JD PhD. Mr. Pope wrote a paper with Lindsey Anderson, and that paper educated Alan and me about VSED. Along the way, I became acquainted with Dr. Timothy Quill. As a well-known and respected palliative care doctor, he leads the way with end-of-life care. Along with others, Dr. Quill, Thaddeus Pope and I organized and spoke at the first national conference on VSED in October 2016 at Seattle University. Whenever I've written to either of them to inquire about medical or legal information, I've always received prompt and complete answers. They both are dedicated professionals who go beyond the call of duty in their professions as a way to help others.

My deepest love and gratitude go to my mother, Florence, and my husband, Alan. I was privileged to be at their bedside when they both died. They both modeled how to have a good quality of life and a good quality of death.

DISCUSSION GUIDE

1) Phyllis mentions that people are often relieved, after reading the book, to learn that they have more choice at the end of their life than they had realized even if they are facing a disease as horrible as Alzheimer's disease. What is your overall reaction to this? As a result of reading the book, has your view of end of life choices expanded? If so, how?

2) Is VSED a controversial issue for you? If so, why? What is it based on?

3) What new information did you learn from this book? Do you have more questions about this? What are they?

4) What parts of the book surprised you the most?

5) As a result of reading the book, what might you do differently toward the end of your life? Would you like to have a Celebration of Life before you die? Do you have a Health Directive that has been filled out and notarized?

6) How do you feel about Phyllis making her personal story so public?

7) Have you ever been a health advocate for someone who is at the end of their life? What was the experience like for you?

8) Phyllis mentions that other people had strong opinions about Alan's choice and her support of his choice. What is your opinion?

9) Is your own fear of death heightened or lessened as a result of reading this book? Why?

10) Alan said, "Now that I've investigated it, it doesn't sound horrible (VSED) and I'm going to do it. I'm doing it because I have a disease that will rob me of the ability to make this choice." What choice would you hypothetically make if you had Alan's experience and were diagnosed with Alzheimer's disease?

11) Are you living or are you dying? What does this question mean to you?

12) What parts of the author's story can you relate to the most?

13) What were your favorite passages in the book? Why?

14) There is one chapter in the book about Alan's experience with cancer and how he chose not to follow the doctor's prescription for surgery. What do you think you would do if you were in Alan's situation and you were diagnosed with Alzheimer's and then cancer only six weeks later? Would you have had the surgeries or not? If the answer is "no," what would you have done instead?

15) What was the most interesting for you about Alan's 9 ½ day process?

16) What do you think about their doctor's view of Alan's choice and why she stepped forward to help him?

17) Alan and Phyllis had good communication with their doctor. That is a main reason why their doctor came forward to help Alan at the end of his life. Do you have good communication with your doctor? What can you do to improve it?

18) Would you like to be as closely involved with your loved one's passing like Phyllis was with Alan? What preparation is helpful?

19) Why do you think Phyllis' involvement as Alan's advocate helped her to move in the direction of giving birth to herself in a new way?

20) Phyllis talks about how Alan prepared himself emotionally to die. How can you live your life today so that you are more prepared to die well in the future? How can you cultivate more awareness about dying? Is this a new concept for you?